GLOSSARY OF

COMMONLY
USED
RESEARCH
TERMS

POCKET
GLOSSARY *for*
COMMONLY
USED
RESEARCH
TERMS

MICHAEL J. HOLOSKO
University of Georgia School of Social Work

BRUCE A. THYER
Florida State University College of Social Work

Los Angeles | London | New Delhi
Singapore | Washington DC

For information:

SAGE Publications, Inc.
2455 Teller Road
Thousand Oaks, California 91320
E-mail: order@sagepub.com

SAGE Publications Ltd.
1 Oliver's Yard, 55 City Road
London EC1Y 1SP, United Kingdom

SAGE Publications India Pvt. Ltd.
B 1/I 1 Mohan Cooperative Industrial Area
Mathura Road, New Delhi 110 044, India

SAGE Publications Asia-Pacific Pte. Ltd.
33 Pekin Street #02-01, Far East Square,
Singapore 048763

Printed in the United States of America

Library of Congress Cataloging-in-Publication Data

Holosko, Michael J.
  Pocket glossary for commonly used research terms /
Michael J. Holosko, Bruce A. Thyer.
    p. cm.
  ISBN 978-1-4129-9513-9 (paper)
  1. Social sciences–Research–Terminology–Handbooks, manuals, etc.
2. Research–Terminology–Handbook, manuals, etc. I. Thyer,
Bruce A. II. Title.
  H62.H5934 2011
  001.403–dc22   2011004865

This book is printed on acid-free paper.

11 12 13 14 15 10 9 8 7 6 5 4 3 2 1

Acquisitions Editor:	Kassie Graves
Editorial Assistant:	Courtney Munz
Production Editor:	Astrid Virding
Copy Editor:	Pam Schroeder
Typesetter:	Hurix
Proofreader:	Scott Oney
Cover Designer:	Gail Buschman
Marketing Manager:	Helen Salmon
Permissions Editor:	Adele Hutchinson

CONTENTS

PREFACE

We have taught social and behavioral science research and evaluation to baccalaureates, masters, and doctoral students for some 64 years collectively. We believe that the number one barrier to students learning research is their anxiety associated with its language and the terms it uses. We have witnessed many students in research classes afflicted with the well-known diseases of "science-itis," "math-itis," "table-itis," or "jargon-itis." For many, these conditions are not mutually exclusive. For others, they cause nightmares!

If students do not understand the language of whatever subject they are trying to learn, their ability to grasp that subject becomes even foggier. A British scientist recently referred to such difficult language use as *complexification*. For example, how many times have you picked up a research study and tried honestly to read and comprehend it, but it was written in scientific babble that was not understandable to you? Well, you are not alone. Now, think for a moment about how a practicing professional, for example, a social worker, psychologist, teacher, nurse, and so on, who has been out of school (and research classes) for a while may feel when he or she is reading the same article. It is indeed a sad testimony to our legacy as social science researchers and scientists that we do not disseminate knowledge in simpler ways to the very people that (we say) can benefit from its use the most!

It took us 3 years to write and rewrite this glossary, as we worked hard to take technical, 10-cent research terms and put them in 5-cent, everyday language. We are proud of the fact that a great number of these complex terms are presented to you in simple ways. We also pretested this language with samples of high school seniors and undergraduate and graduate students. We passed out highlighters (and pizzas) to these samples, and if they did not understand a word in the phrase, they highlighted it, and we made it simpler. As you can imagine, for many terms, this was a real challenge for us.

Within the glossary, then, you will see many one-sentence definitions, and no definitions are longer than four sentences. When we were compiling terms for this text, we came to realize a few things: (1) this is not a dictionary that requires depth and specificity but a glossary or a simpler way of defining terms; (2) all research and evaluation terms are obviously not included, just the ones that are most commonly used—and each year, we will add more that you tell us should be added; (3) this book's downloadable web feature will make it easy for you to have on your computer or mobile device when you need to understand something quickly; and (4) the book is a resource pocket guide that you can easily toss into your purse or knapsack and take to class with you.

Surely, it is possible to locate numerous research terms on the Internet via Google, Wikipedia, and so on. However, the quality of these entries is uneven and not subject to careful editing and peer review. In today's expansive, light-speed Information Age, it is difficult for individuals to quickly appraise relevant information in a subject area they are likely to be unfamiliar with. Defining simply all major terms and concepts in one volume will, we hope, prove a great time-saver for students, professionals, and researchers, as opposed to having to hop, skip, and print from website to website.

The text is divided into two sections. Section I includes (1) a glossary of terms; (2) a list of commonly used acronyms, symbols, abbreviations, and terms and symbols frequently found in research studies you may be reading; and (3) definitions of frequently used statistical terms. Section II includes a variety of field-tested websites and web resources for research and evaluation that students can access readily. These include websites related to quantitative research, qualitative research, evaluation research, statistics, and additional research-related sites. The final chapter, Chapter 5, provides a rank order listing of the core journals of 13 major fields or disciplines whose readers might use the glossary, as well as a list of the journals' respective URL websites, so you can readily access them. For the latter, we used the standard rankings of the impact of these core journals published in the *Journal Citation Reports, 2008* (published by Thomson Reuters).

The intended primary market for this glossary is undergraduate and graduate students in the social and behavioral sciences. We also hope that practicing professionals who read and conduct research and evaluation can benefit from its simplicity and unique features. In short, it is intended for anyone who wishes to break the language barrier in learning about social research and evaluation and who requires accessible, easy-to-read definitions of research terminology. But alas, we would prefer that you be the judge of that. We leave you now with a quote that inspired this work.

"Everything should be as simple as it is but not simpler."

—A. Einstein

ACKNOWLEDGMENTS

In a text of this nature, there have been many individuals to thank over the 3 years of its incubation. At the University of Georgia, we would like to acknowledge the dedicated work of the graduate student assistants assisting the Berger Chair with this task: Elaine Howse Danner, Chelsea MacCaughelty, Irina Ciurea, Kate Morrisey Stahl, Soonok An, Catherine Patterson, and Suo Deng. Special thanks go to Stacey Kolomer for encouraging the phone application suggestion for this text. The generosity of Dr. Israel Berger offering this Chair, on behalf of his wife Pauline, made a work of this nature possible over a 3-year time span. We also wish to acknowledge the support given by the Tisha Abolt Graduate Assistant scholarship for this text. We want to thank those graduate and undergraduate students who were part of the important sample, volunteered to pretest these terms, and told us frequently to "write them easier" and "write them simpler." Your voices were indeed heard, and your advice was heeded. We want to thank the legions of BSW, MSW, PhD, BA, RN, MA, MSc, and MPH students we have taught collectively over the past 64 years. Yes, you have taught us much more about research knowledge and understanding than we ever taught you. You were, indeed, the inspiration for the perspiration for this text. Another thank-you goes to the various waves of reviewers through Sage Publications who offered constructive comments to move this text to its final form. The senior acquisitions editor Kassie Graves marshaled this work through to its final form and stayed with all of its various iterations with utmost professionalism and a refreshing sense of humor.

To our loving families and spouses, thank you so much for forbidding us to talk about work at home and for keeping our lives balanced and centered.

MJH and BAT

The following reviewers provided feedback at different draft stages:

Lynn Comerford, *California State University, East Bay*
Kathy Duncan, *University of La Verne*
Mack Mariani, *Xavier University*
Peter Marston, *California State University, Northridge*
David F. Rico, *George Washington University*
Darlene A. Thurston, *Jackson State University*

SECTION I

THE GLOSSARY

The major part of this text is a glossary of commonly used research and evaluation terms. It presents approximately 1,060 terms written in 5-cent, not 10-cent, words. We also realized when writing this that it was impossible to include each and every term, so we selected the main terms used in all research studies. If you happen to come across a term that you would like to see defined, please send it to my e-mail address, mholosko@uga.edu, with the subject line: "New Glossary Terms Needed." We will make every effort to then define it in the next edition.

CHAPTER 1

GLOSSARY OF
RESEARCH TERMS

A

A posteriori logic: A Latin phrase literally meaning "from
that which comes after." Proving things from observations,
experiences, research, evidence, or arguing from the effect
to the cause.

AB design: A single-participant time series design in which
repeated measurements are made until stability is pre-
sumably established, called a baseline (A), after which an
intervention is introduced (B), and an appropriate number of measurements are made to gauge the effectiveness
of the intervention. This type of design cannot usually
establish causality.

ABA design: This is the same as the AB descriptive design,
except a second baseline phase (A) is added. This may
allow stronger causal inferences than the AB design.

ABAB design: This is the same as the AB descriptive design,
except that second baseline (A) and treatment (B)
phases are added. Repeated changes in outcomes following
changes in intervention make a greater case for causality.

ABC design: A single-participant time series design in which
measurements are made until the stability of the baseline

(A) is established. Then, an intervention (B) is introduced, the results are measured, and finally, a second intervention (C) is added, and the results are then measured.

ABCB design: This is the same as the ABAB design, except that the second baseline phase is replaced by a modified treatment phase (C).

ABCD design: A single-participant research design intended to create or test hypotheses in which alternate treatments are used. This helps a researcher to understand how different treatments (B, C, and D) influence the client.

Abscissa: This is the horizontal line, or x-axis, on a graph.

Absolute benefit increase (ABI): The absolute arithmetic difference in rates of good outcomes between experimental (EER) and control participants (CER) in a trial, calculated as EER – CER, and accompanied by a 95% confidence interval (CI).

Absolute frequency distribution: A list of the values that a variable takes in a data set. It is usually a list ordered by quantity. It will show the number of times each value appears. The absolute frequency is the total number of occurrences of one variable.

Absolute risk increase (ARI): The absolute arithmetic difference in rates of bad outcomes between experimental (EER) and control participants (CER) in a trial, calculated as EER – CER, and accompanied by a 95% confidence interval (CI).

Absolute risk reduction (ARR): The difference between the control group's event rate, or the proportion of participants responding to the placebo or other control treatments, and the experimental event rate, or the proportion of participants responding to the experimental treatment.

Abstract: A summary of a published article found on the first page beneath the title, which describes the article's most important aspects, including its purpose, methods used, major results, and conclusions.

Access: The ability to gain entry to a database, population, or participants for study.

Accessible population: The group of persons from which the researcher can realistically select participants for a study sample and from which the researcher may generalize findings.

Accidental sampling: This involves the sample being selected from that part of the population that is easy to access. That is, a sample is selected because it is readily available and convenient. This is a nonprobability-based sample, also known as a *convenience sample*.

Accountability: Responsibility to a person, organization, or authority for any research activity.

Accuracy: The degree of precision of a measured or calculated quantity to its actual value.

Achievement test: An instrument or scale used to measure the proficiency levels of individuals in given areas of knowledge or skill.

Acquiescence bias: A category of response bias in which respondents to a survey have a tendency to agree with all the questions or to indicate a positive reaction to them.

Acronyms: Abbreviations that are formed using the initial components in a phrase or name: for example, UN, APA, USDA.

Action or **participatory research:** Identifies a social problem or concern and seeks information about it by planned collaborations with individuals or organizations. This is one of the main methods of qualitative research.

Age: The length of time that an organism has lived. It is often used as a demographic variable in research studies.

Age-equivalent score: A score indicating the age level for which a particular performance range is typical.

Allocation concealment: This occurs when the person who is enrolling a participant into a clinical trial is unaware, or *blinded,* to whether the next participant to be enrolled will be put in the intervention or control group. This occurs when assigning individuals to groups to conduct experiments.

Alternate-forms method: A way of assessing reliability, or the degree to which a test produces the same results over time under similar conditions. This method is done by giving two forms of a test that are as similar as possible to research participants. The scores of the two tests are correlated to yield a coefficient of equivalence, with a high coefficient of equivalence indicating the overall test is reliable in that most or all of the items seem to be assessing the same characteristics, and a low coefficient indicating that the two tests are not assessing the same characteristic. This is a test that standardizes a measuring instrument.

Alternate-forms reliability: The degree to which a test produces the same results over time under similar conditions as measured by the alternate-forms method. This is a test that standardizes a measuring instrument.

Ambiguity: The property of a word, term, notation, sign, symbol, phrase, sentence, or any other form used for communication that can be interpreted in more than one way.

Ambiguity, direction of causal influence: This occurs when it is not clear what is causing what to happen or whether the cause precedes the effect. This is sometimes called the *chicken or egg question.* This is a threat to the internal validity of the findings of a study.

Ambiguous independent variable: This occurs when the independent variable is not clearly and operationally defined so that the study cannot be replicated exactly. This is a threat to the external validity of a study's findings.

American Psychological Association (APA): A scientific and professional organization that represents psychologists in the United States. Most behavior and social science journals use the APA style writing format.

Anamnesis: An oral case history of a medical or psychiatric patient as recalled by that patient. This helps in forming a more complete diagnosis incorporating the patient's perception of his or her problem and how it affects him or her.

Androcentricity: Regarding man or the male sex as central, superior, or primary.

Anecdotal data: Based on casual observations or indications rather than rigorous or scientific analysis.

Anonymity: A result of not having any identifying characteristic, such as a name or description of physical appearance, disclosed to the researcher.

Antecedent variables: A variable that occurs before the independent variable and the dependent variable. The variable relationship formula would look like this: Antecedent variable (interest in cause) → Independent variable (interest group support) → Dependent variable (policy decisions).

Appearance: Outward or visible aspects of a person or thing.

Applied research: Systematic inquiry accessing and using some part of the research community's (the academy's) accumulated theories, knowledge, methods, and techniques for a specific patient-, student-, or client-driven purpose. It is one of the defining characteristics of professional research in education, social work, nursing research, and so on.

Aptitude test: An instrument or scale used to predict performance in a future situation. It's often used as a screening test to determine one's special capacities, for example, an IQ test.

Archival research: A form of descriptive and observational research where the researcher examines the accumulated written documents or records of a culture, for example, diaries, films, novels, newspapers, health data, and so on.

Archives: Records that have been accumulated over the course of an individual's or organization's lifetime. These are forms of secondary data.

Arm: Any part of the treatment group in a randomized clinical trial. Most trials have at least two arms.

Asking errors: These are mistakes that an interviewer makes in altering the questionnaire by consciously or unconsciously omitting certain questions, changing wording or the tone of the interview questions, and so on.

Assent form: A written ethics form that documents agreement to participate by individuals who cannot give consent either because they are minors or because they are legally incompetent. Ethically, such individuals must not be enrolled in the study if they do not want to participate.

Assertive community treatment: A team treatment approach designed to provide comprehensive, community-based psychiatric treatment, rehabilitation, and support to persons with serious and persistent mental illnesses, such as schizophrenia. These are usually in-patient treatments.

Associational research: A general type of research in which a researcher looks for relationships having predictive or explanatory power. Both correlational and causal–comparative studies are examples of this type of research.

Assumption: Any assertion presumed to be true but not actually verified. Major assumptions should be described in one of the first subsections of a research proposal or report. They often underpin how the study is rationalized and conducted.

Attribution: Giving credit for information to the person who discovered it.

Audiences: Groups of people who participate in a show or encounter a work of art, literature, theater, music, or academics in any medium. When writing a research report, a researcher needs to consider who his or her target audience will be so that his or her word choice, methods, and dissemination are appropriate.

Audiotape recordings: Information, such as interview conversations, captured on audiotape. This helps a researcher to remember what was said. Their use requires the ethical consent of the research participants. They are often used in qualitative research.

Audit trails: A chronological sequence of audit records, each of which contains evidence directly pertaining to, and resulting from, the execution of a business process, system function, or research study or investigation.

Author affiliation: Where the author of a research study works or obtains funds to finance the research.

Autonomy: The power to govern oneself and make one's own decisions. It is important for research participants to be ethically respected for this principle during a study.

Autoregressive integrated moving average (ARIMA): This statistic is a Box–Jenkins approach to time series analysis. It tests for changes in the data patterns pre- and postintervention within the context of analyzing the outcomes of a time series design.

Availability sampling: A method of sampling based on participants who are available and willing to participate in the study. This is a nonprobability-based sample.

Average: A number representing the way people score based on a summing of all scores and dividing by the number of persons. It is also called the *arithmetic mean score*.

B

B design: A single-participant design wherein formal measurement begins at the same time intervention is initiated.

BAB design: The same as an ABAB design, except that the initial baseline phase is omitted. It is used to evaluate the impact of a treatment already in place.

Background questions: Questions asked by an interviewer or on a questionnaire that obtain information about a respondent's background (e.g., age, occupation, etc.). These are referred to as demographic or sociodemographic questions and are often treated as independent variables in studies.

Bar charts: A chart with rectangular bars with lengths proportional to the values that they represent. Bar charts are used for comparing two or more values.

Baseline: The plotted record of a series of measurements taken prior to the introduction of an intervention in a time series design. It is used to benchmark how the individual is functioning prior to any change. It is the A phase of the study.

Basic research: Research carried out to increase understanding of fundamental principles of a theory or topic rather than research that is designed to be applied to practical pursuits. This need not be empirical research and is also referred to as pure research.

BC design: A single-participant research design intended to develop an understanding of the potential effects of two different types of interventions (B and C).

BCBC design: Time-lapse, single-participant research that compares two different types of interventions (B and C). It permits stronger inferences than the BC design.

Before–after design: See *one-group pretest-posttest design*, also called a *pre- and posttest design*.

Behavior questions: See *experience questions*.

Behavioral observation code: A written document laying out a number of categories of types of behavior that will be measured for a study and how they will be defined. It is usually done in a single chart, ticking the incidents one is observing, for example, by check marks.

Bell-shaped distribution: The normal way that averages are dispersed with a mean of zero and a variance of one. It is called the bell curve because the graph of its probability density resembles a bell. It is also called the *normal curve*.

Belmont Report: A report created by the former United States Department of Health, Education, and Welfare (later renamed Health and Human Services) in 1979, which established the basic federal ethical principles that still guide the use of human participants for research conduct.

Benchmark: This refers to a standard or point of reference against which program processes or outcomes can be compared, typically used in program evaluation studies.

Beneficence: A primary ethical concern of social research. It refers to both doing no harm to people you are studying and, at the same time, promoting a common good for individuals in the research community because of your study. Its origin in present-day social research in America can be traced back to the *Belmont Report.*

Best practices: A technique, method, process, activity, incentive, treatment, or intervention that is more effective at delivering a particular outcome than another technique, method, process, and so on. These are typically based on empirical studies and findings.

Bias: Having a tendency, prejudice, or preference toward a particular perspective. Six prominent forms of this in social research and evaluation include class, gender, race, cultural, social status, and prestige.

Bibliographies: An alphabetical list of books and other works, such as journal articles or websites, used in a research report.

Biometrics: Also called *biostatistics,* this is the science of collecting and analyzing biologic or health data using statistical methods.

Black box evaluation: Evaluation of program outcomes without the benefit of an articulated program theory or an understanding of why an intervention may work.

Blanket consent forms: General written contracts given to research participants to waive their rights. Blanket consents are not as ethically appropriate as consent forms that are more specific to the particular study being done.

Blind, blinded experiment: A study in which the researchers do not tell the participants if they are being given a test treatment or a control treatment in an effort to reduce bias in the results.

Blind review: A process in which the peer adjudicators of a refereed manuscript are not told the author's identity.

Boolean operators: Terms such as *and, or,* and *not,* used to express the relationship of one term to another when searching electronic databases.

C

Callbacks: A technique where the researcher follows up when conducting a survey by telephone or e-mail to remind participants to complete their questionnaires and to return them in a timely fashion.

Campbell Collaboration: An international nonprofit organization that produces systematic reviews of research evidence and is focused on the fields of social welfare, education, and criminal justice.

Captive audience: A group of people exposed to a study condition that is in some way involuntary. For instance, when an audience is exposed to a commercial at a movie, that audience is a captive audience for the commercial being aired.

Carryover effect: A treatment or condition that transposes from one experiment or phase of an experiment to another. There is a possibility of this whenever subjects perform in more than one experimental condition or are given a treatment and it is stopped and then reintroduced.

Case-control study: A study that involves identifying participants who have the outcome of interest (cases) and participants without the same outcome (controls) and assessing if they had the exposure of interest.

Case-level research design: A study organized to explore a particular intervention with one participant in depth. It focuses on descriptive detail rather than scope and is often used in qualitative research.

Case management: This refers to coordination of services to help meet an individual's social service needs, usually when the person has a health or mental health condition that requires multiple services from providers.

Case series: A report on a series of participants with an outcome of interest. No control or comparison group is involved.

Case study: An in-depth investigation of an individual, group, or institution to determine the variables, and relationships among the variables, influencing the current behavior or status of the participant of the study. This is one of the main methods of qualitative research.

Categorical data, variables: Data (variables) that differ only in kind, not in amount or degree. Nominal data are categorical: for example, female versus male, true versus false.

Categorical level of measurement: See *measurement level*.

Category scheme: A way to organize information under topics, for instance, listing health problems under cardiac, nephrology, respiratory, endocrine, and oncology.

Causal-comparative research: Research to determine the causes for, or consequences of, existing differences in groups of individuals; also referred to as *ex post facto* research.

Causal modeling: This refers to a multivariate statistical procedure that calculates the significance and strength of the relationships among a set of independent variables, as well as the relationship between each independent variable and a dependent variable, usually presented in a path diagram.

Causal questions: Inquiries asking how something affected or influenced something else. They normally explore a problem with a manipulated intervention impacting an outcome.

Causal relationship: The relationship between an event (the cause, usually the independent variable) and the resulting event (the effect, usually the dependent variable), where the second event is considered a consequence of the first.

Causal validity: The degree of certainty to which it can be said that an intervention caused the outcome.

Census: Secondary data collected by the government from every member of a population to determine trends and comparative, updated information.

Census divisions, regions: The nine U.S. census divisions are (1) New England, (2) Middle Atlantic, (3) South Atlantic, (4) East South Central, (5) West South Central, (6) East North Central, (7) West North Central, (8) Mountain, and (9) Pacific. The four census regions are (1) Northeast, (2) South, (3) Midwest, and (4) West.

Central tendency: A measure of where the center of a distribution lies. The three most commonly used indices are mean, or arithmetic average; median, or that number or point that divides the data set in half; and mode, or the most frequently occurring number or value.

Centrality of purpose: Maintaining a focus on the mission or initial intent of the study to assess whether the purpose is threaded throughout the following method, results, conclusions, and implications.

Chance: The likelihood of the occurrence of an event.

Chaos theory: A theory and methodology of science that emphasizes the rarity of general laws, the need for large databases, and the importance of studying exceptions to overall patterns. It looks at random events, sudden changes, reversals, and paradoxical trends.

Cheating: Dishonesty or falsification of any kind with respect to examinations, course assignments, or alteration of records. It would be cheating and unethical, as a researcher, to alter one's hypothesis, after a study was completed, to match the results found.

Checklists: A list of items (e.g., names or tasks, etc.) to be completed, consulted, and then compiled.

Chi-square (χ^2): A nonparametric test of statistical significance appropriate when the data are in the form of frequency counts. It compares frequencies actually observed in a study with expected frequencies to see if they are significantly different.

Citation: A reference to a source of information that could be published or unpublished.

Clarity: The quality of something that is free from obscurity and easy to understand.

Classical experimental design: A design that has four nonmutually exclusive criteria: a comparison or control group; randomization or random assignment to condition; specification of a test or null hypothesis; and manipulation of the independent variable. The objective of this design is to assess the impact of the independent variable(s) on the dependent variable(s). The assumption is that the dependent variable in the experimental group will change in a specific way (the hypothesis) and that the dependent variable in the control group will not change.

Classical notation system: In experimental designs, there are certain symbols used to describe the main features of the designs. These include R, random assignment to condition or treatment; X, exposure to treatment or intervention; and O, observational period of assessment.

Client-Oriented Practical Evidence Searches (COPES): A model that assists evidence-based practitioners in formulating questions for databases that will get them the most applicable questions and results.

Client outcomes: The short- and long-term benefits that people receive from services or interventions by human services organizations. They are typically found in evaluation studies.

Client service delivery system: An organization set up to link community services, like Meals on Wheels or Temporary Assistance for Needy Families, to the people who need them.

Clinical case identification model: A way of diagnosing problems, like those defined by the *DSM-IV Manual,* in which symptoms are compared to norms to create a specified diagnosis.

Clinical cutting points, scores: A benchmark point or score that sets the line where someone is, either in a problem area or not. For instance, if the cutoff for depression is symptoms experienced for 2 months, this is where the distinction will be made.

Clinical evidence: Proof of a theory, or validation of case evidence or effectiveness, that comes from experience in the field rather than from formal research studies or statistical significance.

Clinical practice guidelines: A systematically developed set of standards designed to assist the clinician and participant make decisions about appropriate care for specific clinical circumstances.

Clinical trial: An experiment comparing the effects of two or more health-care interventions. It is an umbrella term for a variety of designs of health-care trials, including uncontrolled trials, controlled trials, and randomized controlled trials. This is also called an *intervention study.*

Closed-ended question: A question with a list of responses from which the respondent chooses an answer, also referred to as a *closed-form item,* for example, yes-or-no answers, or a three-point rating of always, sometimes, or never, and so on.

Cluster diagram: A type of nonlinear graphic organizer that can help systematize the generation of ideas based on a central topic. Using this type of diagram, a researcher can brainstorm a theme, associate about an idea, or explore a new participant. This is also called a *cloud diagram*.

Cluster sampling: The selection of groups of individuals, called *clusters,* rather than single individuals (e.g., counties, schools, agencies). All individuals in a unique group or cluster are purposely included in the sample selected; the clusters are preferably selected randomly from the larger population of clusters. It can be used for selecting both probability and nonprobability samples.

Cochrane Collaboration: An international organization whose aim is to help people make well-informed decisions about health care by preparing, maintaining, and ensuring the accessibility of systematic reviews of professional literature.

Cochrane Database of Systematic Reviews: A database of systematic reviews created by a group of over 11,500 volunteers in more than 90 countries.

Code of ethics: A set of moral principles created by professional associations to provide guidelines for the professional, ethical behavior and conduct of their members, who hold professionally licensed degrees.

Coding: The process of converting information obtained on a participant or unit into values (typically numeric) for the purposes of data storage, reduction, management, and analysis.

Coefficient of determination (r^2)**:** The square of the correlation coefficient (r). It indicates the degree of linear relationship strength between two variables.

Coercion: To compel or force someone to act or think in a certain way by the use of leverage, power, intimidation, threats, or pressure. This is not allowed with research participants, as their participation must be voluntary.

Cognitive interviewing: The administration of draft survey questions while collecting additional verbal information about the survey responses. It is used to evaluate the quality of the response or to help determine whether the question is generating the information that the author intends.

Cohort: A group of individuals sharing certain significant characteristics in common, such as sex, age, time, place of birth, and so on.

Cohort analysis: The separation of each of two groups into component parts and comparing the results of one group with those of another to see if there is a group difference.

Cohort study: An observational study in which a defined group of people (the cohort) is followed over time. The outcomes of people in subsets of this cohort are compared to examine those who were exposed or not exposed (or exposed at different levels) to a particular intervention or other factors of interest.

Collateral observers: People other than the person studied who can provide additional information. For instance, a researcher might both interview a participant about his or her behavior and then also ask his or her roommate or significant others.

Compare-and-contrast questions: Inquiries that lead a person to consider how two or more topics are alike and simultaneously how they are different.

Comparison group: The group in a research study that receives a different treatment from that of the experimental group, a placebo treatment, or no treatment. It is sometimes referred to as the *untreated* or *control group*.

Compensatory equalization, threat: The use of an experimental treatment that has actual or potential value to participants in which authorities or participants may be unwilling to tolerate an imposed inequity in the distribution of the treatment for ethical reasons. This is a threat to the internal validity of the findings of a study.

Compensatory rivalry, threat: This occurs when the comparison group knows what the program group is getting and, therefore, develops a competitive attitude toward them. This is a threat to the internal validity of the findings of a study.

Competent: When an individual has the physical, mental, and emotional ability to answer and understand research questions posed to him or her.

Complete observer: A role that requires a researcher's identity to remain hidden when engaging in a study. The researcher makes observations of the setting by using devices, such as a hidden video camera, or by remaining invisible behind a one-way mirror or a screen to avoid detection unobtrusively.

Complete participant: A researcher who collects data by participating in the daily lives of those he or she is studying. This method is typically used in qualitative research.

Compliance: The act of following orders and adhering to rules and policies. In research, it refers to participants following the protocols for study and data collection procedures.

Composition question: An inquiry that is structured in such a way as to make a research participant give a detailed answer, usually in the form of an essay.

Comprehension: An ability to understand the meaning or importance of something.

Computer-assisted telephone interviewing (CATI): A data collection method in which researchers use random digit dialing to phone potential research respondents, ask questions as directed by the computer, and key the responses directly into the system.

Computerized databases: Information that has been organized and loaded into computer files for retrieval. Census or hospital data are examples of such.

Computerized, interactive voice responses: A type of technology that allows a computer to detect voice and keypad inputs.

Concept: An abstract or general idea inferred or derived from specific instances. Concepts exclude variables that are dimensions of them, which can be operationalized and studied.

Conceptual classification system: Putting data into discrete conceptual categories to analyze them. For example, in quantitative research, factor analysis loads items that hang together empirically in a conceptual category on a scale or instrument.

Conceptual framework: A type of intermediate configuration of variables or aspects of a theory that have the potential to connect to all aspects of inquiry (e.g., problem definition, purpose, literature review, methodology, data collection, and analysis).

Concurrent validity: The degree to which the scores on an instrument are related to the scores on another instrument administered at the same time or to some other criterion available at the same time. This is a test that can be used to validate a measuring instrument.

Confidentiality: Prevention of disclosure, other than to authorized individuals, of a client's proprietary information, investigation findings, or of a participant's identity. It is a requirement of ethical consent to conduct research.

Confirmability: Capability of being tested (verified or falsified) by an experiment or observation.

Confirmatory factor analysis (CFA): The use of factor and item analysis to confirm the underlying dimension(s) in an empirical assessment of the internal structure of a scale, instrument, or measure. It is one of the two main terms of factor analysis, the other being exploratory.

Conflict of interest: A situation in which someone in a position of trust has competing professional or personal interests. The perception of conflict is still a conflict of interest.

Consistency: Logical coherence and accordance with the facts. It refers to a pattern of repetition in answers, questions, use of measurements, observations, and so on.

Constant: A characteristic, variable, or influence that has the same value or impact for all individuals in a study.

Constant comparison method: A technique for analyzing qualitative data in which data in the form of field notes, observations, interviews, and the like are coded, and then each segment of the data is taken in turn, and compared with one or more categories to determine its relevance, and compared with other segments of data similarly categorized.

Constant measurement error: An error that affects all items comprising a group in a similar manner and to a similar magnitude. Repeated errors are caused by a flaw in the system (such as in the calibration of a measuring device), occur in the same direction, and therefore do not cancel each other out. This is also called *systematic error*.

Constitutive definition: Defines a concept with other concepts and constructs, establishing boundaries for the construct under study and stating the central idea or concept under study; for example, dementia in a study could be just cognitive, not behavioral impairment.

Construct validity: The extent to which scores on a particular test represent the actual distribution of the characteristic that the test is supposed to assess. This is a test that standardizes a measuring instrument.

Content analysis: The analysis of recorded human communications, such as books, websites, facts, trends, paintings, or laws. It is most commonly used by researchers in the social sciences to analyze recorded transcripts of interviews with participants or conduct secondary analysis of published materials to discern patterns. It is often used in qualitative research studies.

Content validity: A nonstatistical type of appraisal that involves the systematic examination of the test content to determine whether it covers a representative sample of the behavior domain to be measured. It is concerned with a test's ability to include or represent all of the content of a particular construct.

Context effect: The influence of environmental factors on one's perception of a stimulus; for example, the halo effect refers to a situation in which someone or something is judged good or bad in one category and is then uncritically judged good or bad in other categories.

Contingency coefficient: An index of relationship derived from a cross break or Chi-square (χ^2) table.

Contingency question: A question whose answer depends on the answer to a prior question.

Contingency table: A table used to record and analyze the relationship between two or more variables, most usually categorical variables. Chi-square (χ^2) tables are forms of these.

Continuous data: Data with a potentially infinite number of possible values within a given range, for example, height and weight.

Contradictory evidence: Results that disprove a hypothesis or seem to deny a researcher's assumptions or claims. These should be acknowledged in a research report.

Contraindication: A specific research circumstance when the use of certain treatment in a study could be harmful to participants.

Control: Efforts on the part of the researcher to remove the effects of any extraneous factors, influences, or variables, other than the independent variable, that might affect performance on a dependent variable.

Control event rate (CER): See *treatment effects*.

Control group: The comparison group in a research study that receives standard treatment, placebo treatment, or no treatment rather than being exposed to the independent variable (or experimental treatment).

Control variable: A variable that does not change or is held constant in the study in order to analyze the relationship between other variables without interference.

Convenience sample: A sample that is easily accessible. This does not represent the whole population and may be chosen because of time, availability, or financial constraints. It is also sometimes referred to as a *grab* or *opportunity sample*. This is a nonprobability-based sample.

Convergent validity: The degree to which an operation, instrument, or scale is similar to (centers on) other operations, instruments, or scales, to which it theoretically should also be similar. This is a form of validity of measurement.

Correlated variation: The Darwinian theory, which says the whole system or organization is so tied together during its growth and development that, when slight variations in any one part occur and are accumulated through natural selection, other parts then become modified.

Correlation (*r*): A statistical measure of the degree of association or relationship between or among two or more variables. It can be positive or negative and ranges from −1.00 to 1.00.

Correspondence: Communications between individuals, often through letters, memos, flyers, or e-mails.

Cost-benefit analysis (CBA): An assessment of whether the cost of an intervention is worth the benefit by measuring both in the same units; monetary units are usually used. It is typically used in program evaluation studies.

Cost consideration: When a researcher takes into account what negative results the study might have for participants compared with what benefits will be gained by the study.

Cost-effectiveness or efficiency analysis (CEA): A measure of the net cost of providing an intervention as well as the outcomes obtained. Outcomes are reported in a single unit of measurement. It is typically used in program evaluation studies.

Cost-minimization analysis: When conducting such a study, the researcher needs to measure all costs inherent to the delivery of the therapeutic intervention. If effects are known to be equal, only costs are analyzed, and the least costly alternative is chosen.

Cost-utility analysis: A measure that converts health effects into personal preferences (or utilities) and describes how much it costs for some additional quality gain (e.g., cost per additional quality-adjusted life year, or QALY). It is typically used in program evaluation studies.

Counterfactual condition: Projecting or providing empirical evidence about what would have happened if the intervention program was not offered. It is typically used in program evaluation studies.

Covariation: As the values of one variable change (either increasing or decreasing), the values of the other variable(s) also change. Covariation can be either positive or negative.

Cover letters: Letters sent along with other documents to provide additional information, for example, study purpose, design, and so on, in a survey or research interview.

Cox model: This is a semiparametric statistical technique used to analyze the survival of patients in clinical trials. Using regression analysis, it provides an estimate of the treatment effect on survival after adjustment for other explanatory variables.

Credibility: The quality of being believable or trustworthy.

Criterion-related validity: The extent to which the measurement correlates with an external criterion of the phenomenon under study. A typical way to achieve this is in relation to the extent to which a score on a personality test can predict future performance or behavior *(predictive validity)*. Another way involves correlating test scores with another established test that also measures the same personality characteristic *(concurrent validity)*. This is a test that standardizes a measuring instrument.

Criterion sampling: A procedure whereby cases are chosen that meet the same criterion. It is also called *judgment sampling* and is used in many program or practice evaluation studies. This is a nonprobability-based sample.

Criterion variable: This is the change variable that is impacted by independent variables in the study. It is also called *the main dependent variable*.

Critical appraisal skills: The ability of assessing and interpreting research or evidence by systematically considering its validity, results, and relevance.

Critical thinking: This involves evaluating the various dimensions of a research phenomenon (e.g., study questions, assumptions, methods used, etc.). One then synthesizes, assesses, and analyzes these and appraises their interrelatedness.

Critical value: A value taken from a statistical table. It serves as the criterion for determining whether the corresponding data-based statistic is large enough to be considered as evidence against the null hypothesis.

Cross break table: See *contingency table*.

Cross-population generalizability: The ability to generalize from findings about one group, population, or setting to other groups, populations, or settings.

Cross-population sampling: The process through which a group of representative individuals is selected from multiple populations for the purpose of statistical analyses.

Cross-sectional study: The observation of a defined population at a single point in time or time interval. Exposure and outcomes are determined simultaneously.

Crossover study, design: The administration of two or more experimental therapies, one after the other, in a specified or random order to the same group of participants.

Culture: A set of learned beliefs, mores, values, and behaviors shared by members of a society.

Curiosity: An emotion that is said to cause natural inquisitive behavior, such as exploration, investigation, and learning. All research has the scientific tenet of a driving curiosity.

Current population survey: A snapshot assessment of a trend in the population, for example, a statistical survey conducted by the United States Census Bureau for the Bureau of Labor Statistics (BLS). The BLS uses these data to provide a monthly report on the employment situation, which reports estimates of the number of unemployed people in the United States.

Cutoff scores: The lines dividing the criterion of one diagnostic benchmark from another. For instance, an IQ score of 49 would be part of a diagnosis for moderate retardation, while 50 would signify mild retardation.

D

Data: A collection of information and facts from which conclusions may be drawn. This may consist of numbers, words, or images, particularly as measurements or observations of a set of events, behaviors, or variables.

Data analysis: Reducing empirical data in forms to be better understood and interpreted.

Data collection: A systematic process of gathering information to be studied. This process should be checkable and verifiable.

Data encryption: A method of securing transmitted data through encoding to ensure that sensitive and confidential information remains safeguarded and private.

Data mining: This is the process of revisiting or digging back into collected data for further analysis.

Data points: Individual points where a value can be plotted on a line, a bar, or a pie chart. These are individual pieces of information from which decisions about data sets may be made.

Data recording method: The method of the preservation, collection, or registration of individual elements of information in a study.

Data sets: Collections of information, usually presented in numerical or tabular forms.

Data sources: Documents, people, and observations that provide information for assessment, research, or evaluation.

Database, computer: A collection of information stored on a computer storage medium in a common pool for access on an as-needed basis.

Debriefing sessions: Typically a one-time, semistructured conversation with an individual who has just participated in a study. This provides the individual with information he or she might need to achieve closure, especially if the study has caused emotional or physical stress.

Deception: The act of convincing another to believe information that is not true, or not the whole truth, as in certain types of half-truths. This is not allowed in most research, and when used, it must not cause harm and must usually be approved by an institutional review board (IRB).

Decision analysis, clinical decision analysis: The application of explicit, quantitative methods that quantify prognoses, treatment effects, and participant values in order to analyze a decision under conditions of uncertainty.

Deductive logic: See *deductive reasoning*.

Deductive reasoning: Systematic consideration that begins with a general principle and concludes with a specific instance that demonstrates the general principle. This is the application of a philosophy. It is typical of qualitative research approaches.

Degrees of freedom *(df)*: The number of values in the final calculation of a statistic that are free to vary.

Demographic data: Background information relating to statistical characteristics of human populations (e.g., age, gender, race, income, etc.). These data are typically used as independent variables to subgroup variables to compare cohorts in data analysis.

Demoralization, threat: A potential issue in controlled experiments in which those in the control or comparison group become resentful of not receiving the experimental treatment. Alternatively, the experimental group could be resentful of the control group if the experimental group perceives its treatment as stressful or inferior. This may be a threat to the internal validity of the findings of a study.

Dependability: The importance of the researcher accounting for, or describing, the changing contexts and circumstances of a study. Dependability may be enhanced by altering the research design as new findings emerge during data collection. Dependability is analogous to reliability, that is, the consistency of observing the same finding under similar circumstances. This is fundamental to qualitative research.

Dependent *t*-tests: A data analysis procedure that assesses whether the means of two related groups are statistically different from each other, for example, one group's mean score at time one compared with the same group's mean score at time two.

Dependent variable: What is measured in an experiment and what is affected during the experiment. The dependent, change, or criterion variable responds to the independent variable. It is called *dependent* because it *depends* on the independent variable. In outcome studies, the dependent variable is the outcome measure, and the independent variable the treatment.

Descriptive case-level design: A design in which the major research emphasis is on describing the characteristics of one individual or case. It is often used in qualitative research.

Descriptive-comparative question: An inquiry that asks, "Is group A different than group B?"

Descriptive group-level research, design: A design in which the major emphasis is on describing the characteristics of groups of people, such as families, organizations, and communities. It is often used in qualitative research.

Descriptive research, study: Research that examines in depth situations as they are, identifying characteristics of observed phenomena and exploring possible associations among phenomena. These types of studies cannot determine causal relationships. This is a major classification of quantitative research.

Descriptive statistics: Numbers used to describe the basic features of sample data in a study. They provide simple summaries about the sample and its measures, for example, mean, median, mode, variance, or standard deviation. Descriptive statistics form the beginnings of most quantitative studies' data analysis processes.

Diagram: A pictorial or graphic means of showing all the fields and tables in a database and how they are related.

Diary: A recording of information in the form of chronological events. It may include a logbook or pictorial, printed, or audiovisual notations. This is one of the main qualitative techniques used.

Dichotomy: Any splitting of a whole into two nonoverlapping parts.

Differential research participant selection: A sampling process in which the participants selected for a study are different from one another to begin with in some way that is significant for the study. This can be a problem if researchers cannot randomly assign participants to groups and instead are forced to use preexisting groups.

Diffusion of treatment, threat: This occurs when a comparison group learns about a research program from other program participants, keeping the control and experimental groups from remaining distinct. This may be a threat to the internal validity of a study.

Direct costs: The actual dollar costs associated with the operation of a program, including all operating and support costs noted on the program's budget.

Direct observation: A research technique in which a researcher watches and records behaviors or events as they actually occur.

Directional hypothesis: One type of hypothesis or educated guess about what the results of a study will be, predicting the way that the independent will affect the dependent variable.

Discreditable group: Those who possess qualities that are not acceptable to members of the dominant culture. This power dynamic is important to understand in conducting research with disempowered groups, for example, vulnerable populations, involuntary or captive samples, and so on.

Discrete variable: A variable that takes values from a finite or countable set, such as the number of days one stayed in a hospital in a year.

Discriminant validity: The degree to which the operationalization is not similar to (diverges from) other operationalizations that it theoretically should not be similar to. A successful evaluation of discriminant validity shows that a test of a concept is not highly correlated with other tests designed to measure theoretically different concepts. This is a form of validity of measurement.

Discrimination: Unfair treatment of a person or group on the basis of prejudice or biases, either stated or implied.

Discussion of findings: The subsection near the end of a scientific paper or research report that pulls all of the information together. It typically uses previously collected literature to corroborate or refute the results found in a study.

Disinterestedness: Freedom from bias or selfish motives. A researcher should cultivate this principle.

Disproportionate stratified sampling: A sampling method in which the proportion of the groups in the sample purposely does not match the proportions in the population. A typical use is oversampling of certain subpopulations (e.g., African Americans) to allow separate statistical analysis of adequate precision. This is usually a nonprobability-based sample.

Dissemination of research findings: Publishing the results of a research study to public forums to impart knowledge.

Divergence: The evolution of increasing difference between lineages in one or more factors or characteristics.

Diversity: The variation in society of culture and other factors, including differences in age, race, gender, disability, physical abilities, sexual orientation, religion, and so on.

Double-barreled questions: A question that lends itself to two concurrent possible responses, for example, "Do you plan to retire early, and do you have good health?" Surveys must avoid such *and* questions, as when answered, it is not known which part of the question is being responded to.

Double-blind experiment: An especially strict way of conducting a research experiment, usually on human participants, in an attempt to eliminate participant bias on the part of both experimental participants and the experimenters. In a double-blind experiment, neither the participants nor the researchers know who belongs to the control group and who belongs to the experimental group. Only after all the data have been recorded (and, in some cases, analyzed) do the researchers learn which individuals are which.

Double standard: Refers to one class of entities being treated differently from another class of entities and implies an unfair or unjustified differentiation. It sometimes exists in comparison-treatment group studies.

Dropout rates: The number of research participants who quit participating in the study before the study is complete, sometimes referred to as *attrition*.

E

Ecological research perspective: A perspective of research that focuses on interrelational transactions between systems and stresses that all existing elements within an ecosystem play an equal role in maintaining the balance of the whole.

Ecological survey: A collection of information based on aggregate data for some population as it exists at some point or points in time; it's used to investigate the relationship of an exposure to a known or presumed risk factor for a specified outcome.

Economic efficiency: The net social value of a project or program, estimated by subtracting the discounted social costs from the discounted social benefits. It is typically used in program evaluation studies.

Effect size (ES): An index used to indicate the magnitude of an obtained change or result or relationship between time one and time two observations. Cohen's *d* is the most commonly used statistic to compare mean score differences. Approximately speaking, ESs can be small, < 0.3; medium, = 0.5; or large, > 0.75.

Effectiveness study: A study evaluating a treatment, conducted under clinically representative, or real-life, conditions. It is usually used in the later stages of evaluating a new intervention.

Efficacy, drug or treatment: The maximum ability of a drug or treatment to produce a result regardless of dosage. The Food and Drug Administration (FDA) mandates that clinical trials go through three sequential phases of efficacy testing prior to their administration.

Efficacy study: A study conducted under conditions of maximum experimental control (e.g., carefully screened clients, highly trained therapists using detailed treatment manuals).

Efficiency: The degree to which outcomes are achieved in terms of input and resources allocated. Efficiency is a measure of performance in terms of which management may set objectives and plan schedules and for which staff members may be held accountable. It is typically used in program evaluation studies.

Electronic database: Files of information for research access that have been stored through electronic methods, such as a CD, DVD, or jump drive or in an online format.

Electronic survey: A method of gathering information from respondents over the Internet, such as through e-mail or instant messages, or by using LISTSERVs to contact study respondents.

Element: One of the simplest or essential parts or principles of which anything consists or upon which the constitution or fundamental powers of anything are based.

Empathy: The capacity to truly recognize or understand another's state of mind or emotion that is seen or sensed.

Empirical: Based on observable and checkable evidence. It relies on the replication of findings and systematic observations gathered using certain standards of evidence.

Empiricism: A pursuit of knowledge purely through experience, especially by means of observation and also by experimentation.

Encryption: Any process for disguising information to protect it from unauthorized viewing or use. It is often used for files transmitted over the Internet to safeguard confidentiality.

Environmental factor: A factor in the surroundings of a program that may have an effect on it and on the intended outcomes, for example, the demographics of a community.

Environmental scan: An analysis of trends and key factors in an organization's environment that may have an impact on it.

Epidemiology: The study of the health of populations and communities, not just particular individuals. That branch of medicine or public health that deals with the study of the causes, distribution, and control of disease in communities or populations.

Epistemology: A branch of philosophy that investigates the origin, nature, methods, and limits of human knowledge.

Equipoise: A state of uncertainty where a person believes it is equally likely that either of two treatment options is better.

Equivalent forms method: A way of checking consistency by correlating scores on similar forms of an instrument taken by the same participant. It is also referred to as *alternative-forms reliability* and *equivalent-forms reliability*. This is a test that standardizes a measuring instrument.

Error of central tendency: A rating error occurring when the rater displays a propensity to assign only average ratings to all individuals being assessed.

Error of measurement: The difference between the actual value of a quantity and the value obtained by a measurement. Repeating the measurement may improve (reduce) the random error (caused by the accuracy limit of the measuring instrument) but not the systemic error (caused by incorrect calibration of the measuring instrument).

Estimation, statistical: Estimation is the process by which sample data are used to indicate the value of an unknown quantity in a population. Results of estimation can be expressed as a single value, known as a *point estimate*, or as a range of values, known as a *confidence interval (CI)*.

Ethical issue: A question concerning what is moral or right. All research must be scrutinized for the safeguarding of ethics of its participants and experimenters who conduct the research.

Ethnicity: Identifying characteristics shared by a group, such as culture, custom, race, language, religion, or other social distinctions.

Ethnocentrism: The tendency to look at the world primarily from the perspective of one's own culture or heritage.

Ethnography, ethnographic research: Studying cultures to learn more about their interactions, values, meanings, behaviors, language, and worldview. This is one of the main methods of qualitative research.

Evaluation: A systematic assessment of merit, worth, and significance of something or someone based on a set of standards.

Evaluation assessment: A study of the options for conducting an evaluation of a program, including the purpose, proposed methods, stakeholders, and dissemination plan. It is also called an *evaluability assessment*.

Evaluation research: A systematic inquiry to describe or assess the intervention impact of a specific program or intervention on individuals by determining its activities and outcomes. These can be evaluations of practice or programs.

Event history analysis: This is also called *survival analysis, duration analysis, hazard model analysis, failure–time analysis,* or *transition analysis.* It is an umbrella term for a set of procedures for time series analysis and is used in studies where the phenomenon of interest is duration-to-event, where events are discrete occurrences. It computes data units with time, changes, and factors influencing them. It can be parametric, semiparametric, or nonparametric.

Event rate: The proportion of research participants in a group in whom the event is observed. Thus, if out of 100 participants, the event is observed in 27, the event rate is 0.27. *Control event rate (CER)* and *experimental event rate (EER)* are used to refer to this in control and experimental groups of participants, respectively. The *participant expected event rate (PEER)* refers to the rate of events we would expect in a participant who received no treatment or conventional treatment.

Evidence-based health care: Work that extends the application of the principles of *evidence-based medicine (EBM)* to all professions associated with health care, including purchasing and management.

Evidence-based medicine (EBM): The conscientious, explicit, and judicious use of current best evidence in making decisions about the care of individual participants. The practice of evidence-based medicine requires the integration of individual clinical expertise with the best available external clinical evidence from systematic research and the patient's or client's unique values and circumstances.

Evidence-based practice (EBP): See *evidence-based medicine,* except applied to areas distinct from health care, such as social work, public policy, administration, supervision, or community practice. EBP may be applied to all areas of practice, micro through macro.

***Ex ante* evaluation:** An evaluation that is conducted before a program is implemented. It is typically used in program evaluation studies.

***Ex post* evaluation:** An evaluation conducted after a program has been implemented. It is typically used in program evaluation studies.

Exchangeability: A statistical concept in which two factors may be changed without affecting the results. The factors may be, for example, the throws of a coin. Such throws are exchangeable if the order in which they are done is irrelevant for the probabilities of possible outcomes—the probabilities being the results.

Executive summary: A brief overview of the project's purpose, scope, methods, results, conclusions, findings, and recommendations. It is typically placed at the beginning of the research study or technical research report.

Existence question: An inquiry about whether something still exists or there is nothing.

Existing knowledge: Information that already is available about a topic. This can be drawn upon for literature reviews, questioned, and possibly reinforced or refuted by research. It is also referred to as *extant knowledge*.

Expected frequency: This is a theoretical, predicted occurrence obtained from an experiment to be true, unless statistical evidence in the form of a hypothesis test indicates otherwise.

Experience: The accumulation of knowledge or skill over time, which is used to advance an understanding of something.

Experience question: An inquiry by a researcher in a study to find out what sorts of things an individual is doing or has done, which could shape his or her answers to other questions.

Experiment: A research study in which one or more independent variables is systematically varied by the researcher to determine its effects on dependent variables.

Experimental design: A research method that tests the relationship between independent (treatment) and dependent (outcome) variables. In nomothetic research, a true experimental study must meet all of the following criteria: (1) randomization, (2) a manipulated treatment condition (X), (3) a comparison or control group that does not receive any treatment condition, and 4) a specification of hypotheses.

Experimental event rate (EER): The proportion of participants in the experimental treatment group who are observed to experience the outcome of interest.

Experimental group: The group in a research study that receives the treatment (or method) of special interest in the study.

Experimental rigor: This describes a well-designed research study conducted in a methodologically sound way, which follows proper scientific and ethical protocols.

Experimental variable: The factor or treatment condition that is manipulated (systematically altered) in an intervention study by the researcher.

Experimenter bias: See *experimenter expectancy, threat*.

Experimenter expectancy, threat: When the biases of individuals conducting a study influence the outcomes. It is also referred to as *experimenter bias*. This is a threat to the internal and external validity of the findings of a study.

Explanatory design: A research design in which the researcher attempts to identify cause-and-effect relationships.

Exploration: To study in depth a phenomenon, event, population, intervention, interaction, culture, and so on, in order to acquire more knowledge about it.

Exploratory case-level design: A study that examines in detail one intervention, providing information about how well that treatment intervention is working and indicating whether a client's problem has been resolved. When studies with this design are compiled, success of a program can be gauged.

Exploratory design: A research design in which the researcher investigates an area in which little information exists. The aim is to gain more information before doing more thorough research. Often, this design helps researchers to learn to ask the right questions as an outcome of their conduct. It is sometimes referred to as a *level one study*.

Exploratory factor analysis (EFA): A statistical technique that explores the underlying factor structure of a set of observed variables without imposing a preconceived structure on the outcome. It is often used in developing an instrument or measurement scale and is one of the two main forms of factor analysis, the other being confirmatory factor analysis.

Exploratory group-level research design: The arrangement of a type of study that explores a research question about which little is already known in order to uncover generalizations and develop hypotheses that can be tested later with more precise and more complex designs and data-gathering techniques. In this type of design, the effects of one intervention on a group are observed and recorded.

Extant knowledge: See *existing knowledge.*

External criticism: Feedback received from a colleague who is uninvolved in a research project about how to make the project better.

External generalizability, threat: The extent to which the results of an evaluation or research study can be generalized to other times, other people, other treatments, and other places. This is a threat to the external validity of a study.

External validity: The extent to which the data collected from a sample can be generalized to the entire population from which the sample was drawn.

Extraneous event, threat: A happening that occurs during the course of a study that can affect the responses of participants, independent of the experiment. This is a threat to the internal validity of a study.

Extraneous question: An inquiry that is not pertinent or relevant to what is being studied. This sometimes happens when a researcher gets sidetracked in a research interview.

Extraneous variable: A factor or condition, other than that being studied, that makes possible an alternative explanation of results; an uncontrolled or rival variable.

F

F-test: A statistical test of the equality of the variances of two or more populations. The test compares the differences between groups and within groups over time. It is used in analysis of variance inferential tests (ANOVA).

Face-to-face interview: A method of gathering information from participants that involves gathering data by asking the participant specific study questions.

Face validity: The appearance by simple visual inspection that a measurement device assesses what it is supposed to measure.

Factor analysis: A multivariate technique that analyzes the underlying structure of a data set. It is useful in explaining observed relationships among a large number of variables in terms of simpler relations. It is also used to develop a new scale or instrument. Two main forms are exploratory and confirmatory.

Factorial design: An experimental design involving two or more independent variables, at least one of which is manipulated in order to study the effects of the variables individually, and in interaction with each other, upon a dependent variable.

Factorial validity: The degree to which the measure of a construct conforms to the theoretical definition of that construct in a scale or instrument being used or analyzed. This is a test that standardizes a measuring instrument.

Fail-safe: A device or feature that prevents total failure in the event of a fault occurring in a study.

False positive: A result that is erroneously positive when a situation is normal; for example, a pregnancy kit is used and its results are positive, but the woman is not pregnant.

Feedback: The return of information about the results of a process.

Feeling-type question: An inquiry by a researcher that seeks information about a person's attitudes, beliefs, motives, and emotions. Generally, feeling-type questions will generate more in-depth responses. They are typically used in qualitative research.

Feminist research: A body of research oriented to study the social conditions and concerns of women in society from a female gender perspective, usually conducted by women.

Field diary: A personal statement of a researcher's opinions about people and events he or she comes in contact with during research, written in a logbook type of document. This helps qualitative researchers remember information gathered as they observe or interact with research participants.

Field jotting: Quick observational notes taken by a researcher; typically used in qualitative studies.

Field log: A running account of how a researcher plans to, and actually does, spend his or her time in the field.

Field notes: The information researchers write down about what they observe and think about in the course of a study, especially in qualitative research studies.

Field research: A study conducted in a natural-setting, physical location, *in situ,* as opposed to research conducted in a laboratory or other contrived setting.

Figure: Data represented in a pictorial form, graph, or visual model.

Filter question: A question in a survey to ensure that respondents meet the required criteria for a subsequent question (or questions) in the survey.

Findings: The outcome of a research study; literally, what was found.

First-level coding: A behavior coding method that employs a systematic analysis of verbal interactions between an interviewer and a respondent. Its purpose is to identify overt problems by quantifying interviewer and respondent behaviors that connote difficulties in both asking and answering survey questions. Typically, this is accomplished by limiting the analysis to the first level of interviewer and respondent interactions because major problems present themselves when the question is first asked and when respondents initially react or respond.

Firsthand data: Information collected directly from a source rather than, for instance, a record of the source.

Fisher's Student *t*-test: A comparison of mean scores from independent or paired samples that follow a Student's *t* distribution.

Fixed-choice question: A form of inquiry that can normally be answered using a simple *yes* or *no,* a specific simple piece of information, or a selection from predetermined multiple choices. It is also called a *closed-ended question.*

Flexibility: The extent to which, and the rate at which, adjustments to changed circumstances are possible in a research study.

Flowchart: A graphic representation of the major steps in a process, system, or relationship between events.

Focus group: An organized discussion with specifically selected individuals to gain unique information about a particular topic. This is one of the main qualitative techniques used.

Focused interview: A discussion with research participants during data collection, organized around several predetermined questions or topics, but providing some flexibility in the sequencing of the questions, and without a predetermined set of response categories or specific data elements to be obtained.

Follow-up study: An investigation conducted to determine patterns of findings or results after some period of time.

Foreshadowed problem: The anticipation of what the research problems in an investigation will be, typically, before they arise.

Formative evaluation: An assessment designed to provide feedback and advice for improving a program. It is conducted to adjust and enhance interventions and is typically used in program evaluation studies.

Frame of reference: A set of assumptions, ideas, and standards that form a viewpoint from which ideas may be evaluated or researched, for example, philosophical, religious, empirical, and so on.

Frequency distribution: A method of showing actual results, often presented as lists ordered by quantity (high to low), indicating the number of times each value appears for a sample. It is a descriptive statistic.

Frequency polygon: A graphical device used for understanding the shapes of distributions. It serves the same purpose as a histogram but is especially helpful in comparing sets of data. A frequency polygon is also a good choice for displaying a cumulative frequency distribution.

Frequency recording: An exact count of how many times a specific behavior occurs.

Frequency table: This is a way of summarizing a data set. It records how often each value (or set of values) of the variable in question occurs. It may also include the percentages that fall into each category. It summarizes categorical, nominal, and ordinal data.

Funneling technique: Conducting an interview beginning with broad general questions and moving to narrower, more specific, and possibly more sensitive, questions.

Futuristic research: Also called *futures research*, this refers to a multidisciplinary branch of operations research whose aim is to conduct long-range planning based on forecasting from mathematical models, cross-disciplinary treatment of a subject matter, systematic use of expert judgments or opinions, and a systems analytical approach.

G

Gain score: The difference between the pretest and posttest scores of a measure in a study. It is also known as a *change score*.

Galileo: An online search engine used primarily for academic searches in libraries.

Game theory: A branch of applied mathematics that is used in the social sciences. It attempts to mathematically capture behavior in strategic situations in which an individual's success in making choices depends on the choices of others.

Garbage in, garbage out: A concept borrowed from computer information processing used primarily to call attention to the fact that computers will unquestioningly process the most nonsensical of input data and produce nonsensical output. It was most popular in the early days of computing but still applies today when computers can yield large amounts of information in a short time.

Gatekeepers: People who can help individuals to form connections with larger groups of community members.

Gender: The socially constructed roles, behaviors, activities, and attributes that a particular society considers appropriate for men or women.

General reference: A source that a researcher uses to identify more specific references (e.g., indexes, abstracts).

Generalizability, threat: The extent to which researchers can apply results from the experimental sample to the accessible population. This may be a threat to the external validity of a study's findings.

Generalizing: This refers to whether the method or findings of the study can be used or replicated in another study.

Genuineness: The quality of being truthful to one's self and others. This is an important ethical principle of researchers and evaluators.

Geographic location: The physical place or locale of something.

Goal: A broad statement of aims or intended outcomes for a program typically used in program evaluation studies.

Goal Attainment Scale (GÀS): This measures the achievement of treatment or intervention goals. When totaled, they produce a Goal Attainment Score (GAS), allowing one to track the progress of people in treatment.

Gold standard: A colloquial phrase used in research to describe the method, procedure, or measurement that is accepted as being the best available, against which data should be compared. It is often referred to as the *benchmark*.

Goodness-of-fit: A test of a statistical model that describes how well it fits a set of observations. Measures of goodness-of-fit typically summarize the discrepancy between observed values and the values expected under the model in question. Such measures can be used in statistical hypothesis testing, for example, to test for normality of residuals, to test whether two samples are drawn from identical distributions as with the Kolmogorov-Smirnov test, or to test whether outcome frequencies follow a specified distribution as with Pearson's Chi-square test.

Google Scholar: An online search engine that specifically searches scholarly articles and books.

Government report: Information put out by public agencies, such as the National Institute of Health (NIH).

Grade equivalent score: A score that indicates the grade level for which a particular performance (score) is typical.

Graph: A diagram displaying data, in particular showing the relationships or patterns between two or more variables pictorially.

Gray literature: This refers to the kind of research material not published in easily accessible journals or databases. It includes things like conference proceedings, abstracts, or research presented at conferences, newsletters, unpublished theses, and so on. It can be in both print and, increasingly, electronic formats.

Grounded theory: The systematic generation of data-based theory to develop explanations, hypotheses, concepts, typologies, meanings, and descriptions of phenomena. This is one of the main methods and requirements of qualitative research.

Group-administered questionnaire: A written survey generally administered to a sample of respondents in a group setting (for instance, to a focus group or students in a class), generally guaranteeing a higher response rate from a very specific group of people.

Group research design: A way of organizing a study that evaluates the effects of an intervention by comparing the results obtained from a group of clients who received an experimental treatment to a group who received no treatment, an alternative treatment, or a placebo treatment.

Grouped frequency distribution: An arrangement of scores, from highest to lowest, in which scores are grouped together into equally sized ranges called class intervals.

Grouping variable: A characteristic of a sample that is used to categorize participants together. For instance, income is a variable that individuals might be grouped around (high, medium, and low).

Guesstimate: A scientific hunch about any part of a research study based empirically on prior experience, literature, best practices, data patterns, observations during the study, clinical significance, anecdotal data, and so on. It is a morphed term combining *guess* and *estimate*.

Guided discussion: An interview in which, rather than asking direct or specific questions, a researcher asks more general questions to get a sense of what the respondent knows.

Guttman scale: A questionnaire that presents a number of items to which the person is requested to agree or not agree, typically done in a yes-or-no dichotomous format. The intent of the scale is that the person will agree with all statements up to a point and then will stop agreeing. The scale may be used to determine how extreme a view is, with successive statements showing increasingly extremist positions.

H

Halo effect, threat: The tendency to consider a person good (or bad) in one category and then to make a similar evaluation in other categories. For instance, if someone is physically attractive, one might also assume (truly or falsely) that the person is also smart.

Hawthorne effect, threat: A positive effect of an intervention resulting from the participants' knowledge that they are in some way receiving special attention.

Helsinki Declaration of 1964: A document containing a set of ethical principles for the world medical research community regarding human experimentation. It was developed in Helsinki by the World Medical Association (WMA) and is widely regarded as the cornerstone document of human participant research ethics. It has been revised six times, most recently in 2008.

Hermeneutics: The study of interpretation theory, as in interpreting the meaning of certain texts.

Heterogeneity: This occurs when there is more variation between the study results (in a systematic review) than would be expected to occur by chance alone.

Heterogeneity of irrelevancies: The theory that, even though there will be a number of random errors and variations in response sets, these inaccuracies will be different from each other and so can be considered to cancel each other out.

Heterogeneity, statistical: This is used two ways: (1) to describe the degree of variation in the effect estimates from a set of studies, or (2) to indicate the presence of variability among studies beyond the amount expected due solely to the play of chance.

Hierarchical Linear Modeling (HLM): A type of regression model used frequently for educational data sets. With this type of data, HLM is often used, as it takes the issue of correlated errors into consideration and provides more realistic and conservative statistical testing. HLM considers sources of errors more rigorously than Ordinary Least Squares (OLS) regression testing.

Hierarchy of evidence: The relative authority of various types of research information. Although there is no single, universally accepted hierarchy of evidence, there is broad agreement on the relative strength of the principle types of research. For example, in determining the effects of an intervention, randomized controlled trials (RCTs) rank above quasi-experiments, while expert opinion and anecdotal experience are ranked even lower. Some evidence hierarchies place systematic reviews and meta-analyses above randomized controlled trials because these often combine data from multiple randomized controlled trial studies and possibly from other study types as well.

Histogram: A graphic representation, consisting of bars or rectangles, of the scores in a distribution; the height of each indicates the frequency of each score or group of scores.

Historical account: Using information from the past to research the phenomena of study.

Historical-comparative research: Systematically studying past questions and events using methods of research or evaluation to inform possible outcomes and answers to current questions and events.

Historical data: Information about events that happened in the past or research results that were collected in the past. These are deemed secondary data.

Historical research: The systematic collection and objective evaluation of data related to past occurrences to determine causes, effects, or trends of those events that may help explain present events and anticipate future events.

History, threat: A specific event occurring between the first and second observation that may impact the dependent variable score change. This may be a threat to the internal validity of the findings of a study.

Holistic approach: Seeking patterns that provide an overall understanding of the evaluation data, including and integrating the perspectives of different stakeholders. It is typically used in program evaluation studies.

Home interview: A series of questions asked to a research participant in the place where he or she resides rather than in an office or laboratory.

Home page: The main or first page of a website, typically with hyperlinks to the other pages on the site.

Homogeneity: A state or quality of being relatively similar or comparable in kind or nature. It refers to data sets, variability, samples, or statistical information.

Human participant research: Studies involving people. This type of study is an important part of social science research and has particular ethical requirements guiding its conduct.

Hypothesis: A tentative, testable assertion regarding the occurrence of certain behaviors or events; a prediction of study outcomes. It is used to determine how independent and dependent variables can be tested and can be written in either null or directional form. It is based on literature, theory, an educated guess, or observation of a phenomenon. It forms the basis of experiments designed to establish plausibility, association, prediction, or causality.

Hypothesis testing: A statistical procedure that involves stating something to be tested, collecting data, and making a decision as to whether the statement should be accepted as true or rejected.

I

Identifying information: Typically demographic or background data that includes an individual's identity, such as last name, address, social security number, or detailed family history. Researchers must be ethically mindful to keep this information confidential.

Idiographic research: Studies concentrating on specific cases and the unique traits or functioning of individuals rather than on broad generalizations about human behavior.

Idiosyncratic variation: Unusual, unexplained, or unexpected individual results in a study that are different than the general findings.

Impartiality: An inclination to weigh multiple views or opinions equally.

Implementation, threat: The possibility that results are due to variations in the way that the intervention is conducted in an intervention study. This may be a threat to the internal validity of the findings of a study.

Implied purpose: An intention behind the stated aim of the study. It is also called the *unstated* or *implicit purpose*.

In-depth interview: Using a structured, semistructured, or open-ended interview to collect data in a research study. These may include using standardized or nonstandardized questions, measurement scales, and so on. This is one of the main qualitative techniques used.

In-person survey: Asking study questions in a face-to-face manner with the respondent.

In situ: A naturally occurring situation or setting in a person's life. Research may be conducted in artificial settings, such as laboratories, or *in situ*, in participants' natural environments.

In vitro: Occurring in the laboratory or outside the body.

In vivo: A Latin term meaning "in life," this refers to occurrences or observations that take place in a participant's natural environment. In clinical medical studies, this refers to *inside the body.*

Incentive: A tangible or intangible reward designed to motivate persons or groups to participate as respondents or participants in a study.

Inception cohort: The group of research participants who are in the study at the beginning before any leave the study for any reason.

Incidence: The proportion of new cases of the target event or behavior in the population studied during a specified time interval.

Inclusion or exclusion criteria: These are the criteria that determine whether a person may or may not be allowed to participate in a research study. They include age, gender, disease type, concurrent disorders, treatment history, and so on.

Incremental effect: A small change noted that occurs over time in the outcomes during the course of a program or practice evaluation study.

Independent variable: The variable that affects or is presumed to affect the dependent variable under study and is included in the research design so that its effect can be determined. This is sometimes called the *experimental, manipulated,* or *treatment variable,* or in outcome studies the *treatment* or *intervention.* In a scientific experiment, you cannot have a dependent variable without an independent variable.

Indexing: The act of classifying information in order to make items easier to retrieve.

Indication: A medical term referring to a sign, symptom, or condition that leads to the recommendation of a treatment, test, or procedure.

Indicator: A measurable variable (or characteristic) that can be used to determine the degree of adherence to a standard or the level of quality achieved.

Indirect costs: Administrative expenses added to a grant's budget by the host organization. Indirect costs are used to support the operation of the host organization.

Inductive logic: Reasoning from the particular to the general, that is, from several similar studies to a theory.

Inductive or deductive theory, construction cycle: The way scientific knowledge is organized and gathered, with studies contributing to the creation of a theory and then that theory being applied and tested in later studies.

Inductive reasoning: The process of making inferences based on observed patterns or simple repetition.

Inferential statistics: Data analysis techniques for testing how likely it is that results based on a sample or samples are similar to results that would have been obtained for the entire population, for example, χ^2, t-, and F-tests.

Informal interview: A discussion used to gather data for a study. These are usually conducted by qualitative researchers. They do not involve any specific type of sequence of questioning, but resemble more the give-and-take of a casual conversation, to collect data in a more relaxed way.

Information retrieval: The science of searching for documents or data, for example, in PsycINFO or Google Scholar.

Information sharing: The reciprocal exchanging of data, as in reporting, publishing, or sharing a database.

Informed consent: The agreement of a person or his or her legally authorized representative to serve as a research participant with full knowledge of all anticipated risks and benefits of an experiment. It is a requirement of most human participant research ethics.

Institutional review board (IRB): See *IRB*.

Instrument: Any device for systematically collecting data, such as a survey, test, protocol, observation, questionnaire, or interview schedule, and so on.

Instrument decay: Changes in measurement devices over time that may affect the results of a study.

Instrument development: To develop an instrument, scale, inventory, interview schedule, assessment tool, or way of measuring a phenomenon and test its utility for use by others.

Instrumentation: Measuring devices used in collecting data in a study. Many social research studies include multiple measures of various concepts.

Instrumentation error, threat: When changes in obtained measurement are due to the instrument calibration or changes in observers, judges, or interviewers (e.g., greater sensitivity with practice or less observer attentiveness after repeated observations). This may be a threat to the internal validity of the findings of a study.

Intangible costs: Costs that are not easily expressed in actual dollar amounts, for example, one's quality of life.

Intention-to-treat analysis: A method of evaluation for randomized trials in which all participants randomly assigned to one of the treatments are analyzed together, regardless of whether they completed or received that treatment, in order to preserve randomization.

Interaction with treatment effects, threat: The extent to which the intervention differentially affects the experimental participants based on their characteristics.

Interactive voice response: A computerized system that allows a person, typically a telephone caller, to select an option from an audio menu and otherwise interface with a computer system.

Intercoder reliability: The extent to which two or more coders agree on the coding of content variables.

Interjudge reliability: The consistency of a rating between two or more independent scorers, raters, or observers. It is also referred to as *interrater reliability*. This is a test that standardizes a measurement instrument.

Interlibrary loan services (ILL): Services whereby a user of one library can borrow books or receive photocopies of documents that are owned by another library.

Internal consistency method: A procedure for estimating the reliability of scores using one administration of the instrument, such as Cronbach's alpha or split-half reliability. These tests help to standardize a measurement instrument.

Internal consistency reliability: The extent to which all items in a scale or test measure the same concept. This is a test that standardizes a measuring instrument.

Internal validity: The degree to which observed differences on the dependent variable are directly related to the independent variable, not to some other (uncontrolled) variable.

Interobserver reliability: The level of agreement between two or more people viewing the same activity or setting.

Interpretation of results: A researcher's explanation and description of what the findings of a study mean.

Researchers use logic, other findings, literature, and empirical justification, typically, to interpret their results.

Interpretative question: An inquiry that has more than one correct answer.

Interpretative research: Studies in which researchers attempt to understand phenomena through accessing the meanings research participants assign to them. Interpretive methods of research start from the position that knowledge of reality, including the domain of human action, may be, at least in part, a social construction by human actors and that this applies equally to researchers.

Interpreter: A person who mediates between speakers of different languages. It is important to have qualified interpreters if one is working with bilingual clients who speak other languages in research studies.

Interpretive validity check: Inspecting accuracy in interpreting what is occurring to a participant and the degree to which the participant's views, thoughts, feelings, intentions, and experiences are accurately understood by the researcher. It is often used in qualitative research.

Interrater reliability: The extent to which two different researchers obtain the same result when using the same instrument to measure a concept.

Interrupted time series design: Research in which ongoing repeated measurements of the outcomes are made and treatment is introduced at some point, while measurements continue as before.

Interval measurement: When items have an equal distance between them on a measurement scale. This is the third level of measurement.

Interval measurement recording: An observational system that divides a predetermined period of time into a number of shorter sections of time. The observer records whether the targeted behavior occurred in each successive interval.

Interval scale: One measurement scale that, in addition to ordering scores from high to low, also establishes a uniform unit in the scale so that any equal distance between two scores is of equal magnitude. It has all of the properties of its two lower subscales, nominal and ordinal.

Interval variable: A quantitative ordering system in which the numerical differences between adjacent attributes are equal. The system includes a value of zero.

Intervening variable: An independent variable or extraneous variable that can influence the main treatment variable and the dependent variable.

Intervention: A specified, planned treatment or method that is intended to modify one or more dependent variables. It is referred to as the *main intervention treatment* or *manipulated variable.*

Intervention study, research: A general type of research in which independent variables (e.g., treatments) are manipulated in order to study the effect on one or more dependent variables (e.g., outcomes). It is typically used in practice or program evaluation studies.

Interview: A form of data collection in which individuals or groups are questioned orally for a survey. Interviews can occur face-to-face, over the phone, or via the Internet.

Interviewer: A person who conducts an interview, for example, a researcher, research assistant, or data collector.

Interviewer bias: Influence on the answers to questions caused by the presence, attitudes, or actions of the person asking the study questions.

Interviewer distortion: Information gathered by a researcher that is not accurate because of misunderstanding, misreporting, or incorrect observing by the researcher.

Interviewing: The process of questioning an individual to obtain specific information for a research study.

Intraobserver reliability: The reliability of responses obtained from the same observer at different time points.

Intrarater reliability: A type of reliability assessment in which the same assessment is completed by the same rater on at least two occasions.

Intrusiveness: The extent to which an intervention disrupts a research participant's normal life.

Inventory: Another way to describe a scale or measuring device that sets out to assess something.

IP address: A series of numbers that are assigned to devices participating in a computer network.

IQ: A score derived from one of several different standardized tests attempting to measure intelligence, for example, the Stanford-Binet Intelligence Test.

IRB (institutional review board): Also known as an independent ethics committee (IEC) or ethical review board (ERB), an IRB is a committee that is designated to approve, monitor, and review biomedical and behavioral research involving humans with the aim to protect the rights and welfare of the research participants. It is a federal requirement in universities, large organizations, hospitals, and so on.

Item validity: The degree to which each of the questions in an instrument measures the intended variable. This is also referred to as *face validity*.

Iterative: The process of repeatedly applying a function to a series of elements in a collection or set until some condition is satisfied.

IVR (interactive voice response): A phone technology used to provide an interactive set of menu options that a caller selects with a phone keypad, which then offers options for more information.

J

Jacobson's change index: A statistical formula developed by Jacobson and colleagues to assess change from pre- to posttest in clinical samples. It can be used with almost any measure on which one is assessing change. It is also called the Reliable Change Index (RCI).

Jargon: The specialized vocabulary or set of idioms shared by a particular profession or subgroup.

John Henry, threat: John Henry was a worker who outperformed a machine in an experimental setting because he was aware that his performance was being compared with that of the machine. This may be a threat to the internal validity of a study.

Journal: A library periodical that specializes in a specific participant area and publishes peer-reviewed articles.

Judgment sample: This is a purposive sample selected by the researcher highlighting certain characteristics of the population that will be targeted for the sample. This is a nonprobability-based sample.

Justification of a study: The rationale statement in a research report in which a researcher indicates why the research is being conducted and is important to conduct. This usually includes implications for theory and practice.

K

Kendall's Tau (τ): A nonparametric statistic used to measure the degree of correspondence between two rankings and assessing the significance of this correspondence.

Key actors: See *key informant*.

Key concept: The essential idea contained within a published report, which may also be contained in specific key words.

Key informant: An individual who is targeted for data collection because his or her information will provide an accurate and relatively wide perspective on the setting, as well as lead to other sources of information. Key informants are often used in qualitative studies.

Key question: A major issue that needs to be addressed by a research study. Each research report purportedly answers a main driving question.

Key word: A word that helps to show what essential ideas are used in an article. These often are listed after the abstract in APA-style articles and are used to code the article in a database.

Kindling effect: Also called the *kindling hypothesis,* this refers to the repeated occurrence of smaller events over time, for example, stress, alcohol and drug use, and so on, that change or spark the brain's chemistry and impact a person's mental health in negative ways, for example, epileptic seizures, depression, or anxiety. This is opposite to a singular major event, for example, divorce or loss of one's job, which can impact a person similarly.

Knowledge-level continuum: The range of the amount of information that participants in a study are likely to have about a particular topic.

Knowledge question: An inquiry made by an interviewer to find out what factual information a respondent possesses about a particular topic.

Kolmogorav-Smirnov (K-S) **test:** A goodness-of-fit test that is used to decide if a sample comes from a population with a specific distribution. The test is based on the empirical distribution function (EDF).

Kruskal-Wallis one-way analysis of variance: A nonparametric inferential statistic used to compare two or more independent groups for statistical significance of differences.

Kuder-Richardson coefficient of reliability (KR-20): A procedure for determining an estimate of the internal consistency of a test or other instrument from a single administration of the test without splitting the test into halves. The KR-20 is used for dichotomous data. This is a test that standardizes a measuring instrument.

Kurtosis: In probability theory and statistics, it is a measure of the peakedness of the probability distribution of a real-valued random variable. It presents a picture of the shape of a distribution. Higher kurtosis means more of the variance and is the result of infrequent extreme deviations, as opposed to frequent, modestly sized deviations.

L

Latent content: The underlying meaning of a communication. For instance, a professor might say, "You're being quiet today," which is explicitly a description, but the latent content might be, "You ought to participate more."

Leading question: An inquiry that suggests the answer or contains the information the examiner is looking for. This is also called *prompting* or *spoon-feeding.*

Level of confidence: The percentage of instances that a set of similarly constructed tests will capture the true mean (accuracy) of the system being tested, within a specified range of values around the measured accuracy value of each test. As a researcher performs more and more tests on a system, he or she becomes increasingly more confident in predicting the result of the next test.

Level of significance: The probability that a discrepancy between a sample statistic and a specified population parameter is due to sampling error or chance. The commonly used significance level in research is $p < .05$.

Life history, calendar: A structured interview utilizing a gridlike format to facilitate recall, on a month-to-month basis, of life events experienced by the interviewee. It can be used to chart behaviors or events for a study and is often used in qualitative research.

Likelihood ratio: The ratio of the maximum probability of a result under two different hypotheses. For instance, the likelihood that a given test result would be expected in a participant with the target disorder compared with the likelihood that this same result would be expected in a participant without the target disorder.

Likert scale: A self-report instrument in which an individual responds to a series of statements on a continuum by indicating the extent of agreement. Each choice is given a numerical value, and the score is presumed to indicate the magnitude of the attitude or belief in the question, for example, all of the time (4), most of the time (3), some of the time (2), and none of the time (1).

Limitation: An aspect of a study that the researcher knows may influence the results or generalizability of the results negatively but over which he or she has little control. These are to be acknowledged in the discussion subsection of a research report. All research has limitations.

Linear relationship: A statistical correlation in which an increase in one variable is associated with a corresponding increase in another variable, and a decrease in one variable is associated with a corresponding decrease in another variable.

Literature review: The systematic identification, location, and analysis of documents containing information related to a research problem. This is usually the subsection before the method, and after the introduction, in a research article. It provides a context for the study.

Location, threat: The possibility that results are due to characteristics of the setting or location in which a study is conducted.

Logbook: Recording information in the form of chronological events in field books, logbooks, case notes, or diaries. These may include pictorial, printed, or audiovisual notations. This is one of the main qualitative techniques used.

Logic: The principle that guides reasoning within a given field or situation. Two main forms of logic prevail in research: inductive, or moving from particular cases to a theory; and deductive, or applying theory to the particular.

Logic model: Developed by the W.K. Kellogg Foundation, this is a way to describe a theory-based rationale for a program and its inputs, activities, outputs, and outcomes. It is typically used in program evaluation studies.

Logistic regression, statistical: It is part of a category of statistical models called *generalized linear models*. It allows one to predict a discrete outcome, such as group membership, from a set of variables that may be continuous, discrete, dichotomous, or a mix of any of these. Generally, the dependent or response variable is dichotomous, such as presence versus absence or success versus failure.

Longitudinal case study design: A way of organizing developmental research in which a case or group is studied repeatedly over a period of days, weeks, months, or years.

Longitudinal one-group posttest-only design: A way of organizing developmental research in which one collection of participants is studied repeatedly over a period of days, weeks, months, or years.

Longitudinal survey: A study in which information is collected at different points in time in order to note changes over time. These studies are usually of considerable length, such as several months or years.

M

Magnitude recording: A list of data that describes the amount, level, or degree of the target problem during each occurrence.

Mailed survey: A questionnaire sent to research participants that they are asked to fill out and to return to the sender, either by post or e-mail.

Management information system (MIS): A system that captures data and turns it into something that is meaningful to help manage activities or decisions.

Manifest coding: A form of coding raw data and transforming it into processed data. It is used in content analyses in which a researcher will count the number of times a particular word or phrase appears in the text or video. It is a reliable method because the word or phrase either appears or does not appear; however, it does not attach meaning to the word or phrase being counted.

Manipulated variable: See *experimental variable*.

Manuscript: A copy of an article or text before it has been printed or published.

Marginal costs: The costs of producing one additional unit of output in a program. Its actual value in dollars is the marginal value. They are typically used in program evaluation studies.

Marketing research: An objective approach to developing studies to answer business management decision-making questions based on target populations.

Matched pairs: Study participants grouped in twos with the comparison group participants. This helps to ensure that the two groups are similar in certain ways; for example, pairs could be matched for age, race, and gender.

Matrix display: A rectangular array of quantities or expressions set out by histograms, bar graphs, or rows and columns.

Matrix questions: A set or series of questions that share answer choices laid out on a grid.

Maturation, threat: The possibility that results are due to changes that occur in participants as a direct result of the passage of time, human developmental processes, or fatigue and that may affect their performance on the dependent variable. This may be a threat to the internal validity of the findings of a study.

Mauchly's sphericity test: This is used to assess the variances in repeated measures ANOVAs (*F*-tests). Sphericity tests whether there is equality of variances of the differences between levels of the repeated measures factor. If this test is not significant ($p > .05$), it is reasonable to conclude that the variances of differences are not significantly different, and thus, the *F*-test can be trusted.

Mean, arithmetic: The sum of the scores in a distribution divided by the number of scores in the distribution. It is the most commonly used measure of central tendency. It is often reported with its companion statistic, the standard deviation, which shows how far things vary from the average.

Meaning unit: The smallest bit of language or numerical information needed to make sense. In the English language, *cat* is a meaning unit; *ca* is not.

Measurability: The quality of being able to be quantified and assessed.

Measurement: The act or process of assigning numbers to phenomena according to a system of valuation.

Measurement error: A degree of inaccuracy in results due to flaws in the measuring instrument.

Measurement instrument: The instrument inventory, scale, or tool used to translate a construct into observable data.

Measurement level: There are four hierarchal levels of measurement. From lowest to highest, these include the following: nominal, or naming variables; ordinal, or rank-ordered variables; interval, or evenly spaced variables; and ratio, or evenly spaced variables where zero has an absolute value. Each level assumes all the characteristics of the ones below.

Measurement of the dependent variable, threat: The extent to which the generalizability of the study's results are limited to the particular dependent measure used. This may be a threat to the external validity of a study's findings.

Measurement scales: See *measurement level*.

Measures of central tendency: A set of descriptive statistics, including frequency, range, percentage, mean, median, mode, variance, and standard deviation of a data set. These are used to find an average, or central tendency of a data set, which refers to a measure of the middle or expected value of the data set. Collectively, they provide a picture of the data set.

Measures of variability: Indices indicating how spread out the scores are in a distribution. Those most commonly used in social science research are the range, standard deviation, and variance.

Measuring instrument: An actual measurement device—observation schedule, diary, logbook, scale, or questionnaire—that shows the extent or amount or quantity or degree of something being assessed.

Mechanical matching: A process of using a computer to pair two research participants whose scores on a particular variable are similar.

Median (*Mdn*): The midpoint or number in a distribution having 50% of the scores above it and 50% of the scores below it.

Mediator variable: This is a variable that describes how rather than when effects will occur by accounting for the relationship between the independent and dependent variables. A mediating relationship is one in which the path relating A to C is mediated by a third variable (B).

Member check: A qualitative research technique in which the interpretation and report (or a portion of it) is given to members of the sample (informants) in order to check the authenticity of the work. Their comments serve as a check on the viability of the interpretation. There are many subcategories of member checks, including narrative accuracy checks, interpretive validity, descriptive validity, theoretical validity, and evaluative validity.

Memory question: An inquiry that gathers information about a research participant's recollection of the past.

Meta-analysis: A systematic review that uses quantitative methods of published research interventions and studies to synthesize and summarize the results of a large numbers of research studies on one particular topic. This allows aggregate claims about interventions and their effects to be made and offers empirical suggestions about best practices of interventions. The unit of analysis in meta-analysis is the effect size found in different studies.

Methodology: The technique used to conduct a study. This is described in detail in a research article. Methodologies are also assessed for their ability to be replicated.

Minority group: People distinguished by being on the margins of power, status, or the allocation of resources within a society; a nonmainstream group in a society or research study. It also includes members of a numerically inferior group.

Mirror sample: A technique used when the researcher suspects that respondents may not tell the truth about their behavior. Instead of asking about the respondent directly, the researcher asks each respondent to think of a close friend of the same sex and age-group. Then he or she asks them to answer for that friend without naming the friend. The theory is that, because they don't know all the details about their friends, they'll really describe their own behaviors. Mirror samples have been used in surveys on sexual behavior and on studies about AIDS. This technique is similar to a third-person technique.

Mixed-mode survey: A way of gathering information that uses multiple ways to obtain information from participants, including strategies such as face-to-face interviewing, online surveys, telephone surveys, and mail surveys.

Mixed research method: Research that combines elements of qualitative and quantitative approaches, for example, completing a study where the first part uses quantitative surveys and the second part uses qualitative interviews and then following up on participants to obtain more open-ended, impressionistic, or detailed data.

Mode (*Mo*): The number that occurs most frequently in a distribution of scores or numbers.

Model: A symbolic representation of the interrelations of variables or factors within a system or a process. It is presented as a conceptual framework or a theory that explains a phenomenon and allows predictions to be made. It is often presented visually or pictorially in a research report.

Moderator variable: A variable that may or may not be controlled but has an effect on the independent or dependent variable.

Monolithic perspective: A perspective that sees the world only in one way.

Mortality, threat: The possibility that results of participants who are, for whatever reason, lost during the course of a study may differ from those who remain. Their absence has important effects on the results of the study. This may be a threat to the internal validity of the findings of a study. It is also referred to as *sample attrition.*

Multicultural research: A systematic study that includes an awareness of race, class, sexual orientation, and other justice issues that influence the way that studies are conducted. This research is interested in, and often critical of, how some systems of reasoning become favored over others.

Multidimensionality: Definitions, constructs, theoretical frameworks, variables, and measurement instruments based on more than a single knowledge area. In social research, these various knowledge areas usually include at least the biological, psychological, sociological, and cultural.

Multigroup posttest-only design: A research design that includes testing whatever intervention is being studied by giving the intervention and then testing after it is given in more than one group.

Multiple baseline design: A single-participant research design in which baseline data are collected on various behaviors for one participant, after which a treatment or intervention is given sequentially over a period of time to each behavior one at a time until all behaviors are under treatment. It is also used to collect data on different participants with regard to a single behavior or to assess sequentially treating a participant's behavior in different settings.

Multiple reality: A theory in phenomenological qualitative evaluation methods that says the world is unique, so people will see it in a number of different ways.

Multiple regression: A statistical technique using a prediction equation with two or more variables in combination to predict a criterion or dependent variable.

Multiple-treatment interference, threat: The carryover or delayed effects of prior experimental treatments when individuals receive two or more experimental treatments in succession. This may be a threat to the internal validity of the findings of a study.

Multiplicity: A large number or variety, usually referring to treatments or interventions.

Mutually exclusive events: Two events are mutually exclusive or disjointed if it is impossible for them to occur together.

N

N-of-1 randomized trials: In such trials, the participant undergoes randomized brief periods of real treatment versus an alternative or placebo treatment. The participant and researcher are blinded, if possible, and outcomes are monitored. Treatment periods are replicated until the researcher and participant are convinced that the treatments are definitely different or definitely not different. It is also known as the *alternating treatments design.*

Naming variables: Giving unique labels to variables so you can easily track them in data analyses.

Narration: Detailed accounts of individuals, events, themes, life histories, and their meanings. These are verbatim accounts from the voices of individuals to the researchers. This is one of the main methods of qualitative research.

Narrative accuracy, check: Taking a study participant's self-report and comparing it to objective factual records or data when possible.

Narrative data: Information gained by listening to a study participant's individual descriptions of an event and recording them verbatim. It is most often used in qualitative research.

Narrative history: Giving an account of events in a story-based form. It is typically used as a qualitative research technique.

Narrative interviewing: A technique involving asking research participants open-ended questions and then recording their answers as they state them to the researcher. It is used primarily in qualitative research.

Narrative review: Opposite of a systematic review, a narrative review is an overview of a person's participative experiences with something that is compiled by a researcher. It is used primarily in qualitative research.

Natural language: A collection of words, phrases, or idioms that are used by people for general-purpose communication, rather than formal or technical communication.

Naturalistic observation: Observation in which the observer controls or manipulates nothing and tries not to affect the observed situation in any way.

Naturalistic research: Studies that observe participants in the environments in which they usually live, rather than in a laboratory setting. This is referred to as *in vivo* or *in situ*.

Naturally occurring settings: Places to research that are not set up or contrived by the researchers but instead already exist and are found and studied by researchers, for example, playgrounds, homes, agencies, churches, or parks.

Naturalness: The quality of faithfully representing nature or life.

Nazi medical experiments: Unethical human experiments conducted by the Nazi party in World War II Germany, which led to stricter international ethical guidelines for researchers worldwide.

Needs assessment: Research or evaluation that seeks to empirically determine what needs are experienced by a client, group of clients, agency, or community. Needs assessment may demonstrate whether a program or intervention is necessary to help solve a problem.

Negative correlation: As the value of one of the variables increases, the value of the second variable decreases. Likewise, as the value of one of the variables decreases, the value of the other variable increases. This is also called an *inverse correlation* and ranges from –1.00 to 0.

Negative (deviant) case analysis: Looking for and talking about information found in a research study that does not seem to support the overall pattern found by the analysis. This is a way to continue to work with data until it can explain the anomaly.

Negative predictive value: Proportion of people with a negative test who are free of the target disorder. See also *likelihood ratio*.

Negatively skewed distribution: A distribution in which there are more extreme scores at the lower end than at the upper or higher end.

Net social value: The economic value of a project or program once net present (discounted) costs have been subtracted from net present (discounted) benefits. It is typically used in program evaluation studies.

Neutral location: A place where power distribution is equal between the people who meet there. For instance, meeting at a professor's office is not neutral, while meeting at a coffeehouse or public park is more neutral.

Nominal measurement: Naming variables, placing them into categories, and assigning numerical values to them for research purposes. The numbers do not reflect anything more than the simple naming of the variable, for example, male = 1 and female = 2. This is the first level of measurement. The three other scales are ordinal, interval, and ratio.

Nominal scale: A measurement scale that classifies elements into two or more categories, the numbers indicating that the elements are different but not according to their order or magnitude (e.g., yes or no; agree or disagree; male or female; or White, Black, or Hispanic).

Nominal variables: Data that are not numbers but are classified using numbers to name them, such as female and male coded as 1 and 2 for data analysis purposes.

Nondirectional hypothesis: A statistical prediction that no relationship exists between two variables (usually) without specifying its exact nature; for example, there is no relationship between one's shoe size and hat size. It is also called the *null hypothesis*.

Nonequivalent control group design: A quasi-experimental design involving at least two groups, both of which may be pretested. One group receives the experimental treatment, and then both groups are posttested. Individuals are not randomly assigned to treatments or conditions, and thus the groups may be different in their makeup or size.

Nongeneralizability dependent variable, threat: This is when the instrument used to measure the dependent variable is not representative of the population of such measures. For example, two anxiety scales may give different results for the same sample. This may be a threat to the external validity of a study's findings.

Nonoccurrence data: Information documenting that something has not happened in a study.

Nonparametric tests, techniques: A body of statistical tests used when the data represent a nominal or ordinal level scale, or when assumptions required for parametric tests cannot be met, specifically in cases of small sample sizes, biased samples, an inability to determine the relationship between sample and population, and unequal variances between the sample and population. This is a class of tests that do not hold the assumptions of normality.

Nonparticipant observations: Observations in which the observer is not directly involved in the situation to be viewed or studied. The researcher tries to stay in the background to be relatively detached from the study.

Nonprobability sample: A subgroup of study participants is selected by the researcher, and it is uncertain if they represent the larger population. These samples can be divided into five main types: availability, convenience, quota, judgment, and purposive.

Nonprobability sampling: Collecting a group of participants in a specific way to study without randomizing their selection.

Nonrandom sampling: The selection of a sample in which every member of the population does not have an equal chance of being selected for a study.

Nonreactivity measuring instruments: Those measures in which a participant's behavior is not influenced by social interaction with the researcher. This refers to the ultimate outcome of an instrument and not the means by which it is achieved.

Nonsystematic observations: Views that have not been researched in a formal or systematic way but are the result of using information as it is presented.

Nonverbal response: Body language, such as looking down at the floor, that communicates something to an observer, even when no words are spoken.

Norm: A descriptive statistic that summarizes the test performance of a reference group of individuals and permits meaningful comparisons of individuals to the group.

Norm group: A sample group used to develop norms or baseline data for an instrument, scale, or inventory.

Norm-referenced instrument: An instrument that permits comparison of an individual score to the scores of a group of individuals on that same instrument or measurement.

Normal curve: A graphic illustration of a normal distribution. See *normal distribution*.

Normal distribution: A theoretical bell-shaped distribution having a wide application to both descriptive and inferential statistics. It reflects the distribution of many human characteristics in typical populations. Measures of characteristics of most individuals and events fall under the higher central part of the bell-shaped curve. The smaller ends of the curve are referred to as the low-chance probability areas.

Normative data: The average for any given test, which helps researchers to understand experimental data to the extent that it differs from what is deemed normal or expected.

Novelty effect, threat: The responses of a study may be partly a function of the newness of the experimental approach. This is a threat to the external validity of the study's findings.

Null hypothesis: A statement that any difference between obtained sample statistics and specified population parameters is due to sampling error or chance. The researcher assumes the testing position that there will be no difference between variables being studied.

Number needed to harm (NNH): The number of participants that, if all received the experimental treatment, would result in one additional participant being harmed compared with participants who received the control treatment, calculated as 1/ARI (absolute risk increase) and accompanied by a 95% confidence interval (CI).

Number needed to treat (NNT): The inverse of the absolute risk reduction (ARR) and the number of participants that need to be treated to prevent one bad outcome. It is calculated as the inverse of the absolute risk reduction (1/ARR).

Nuremburg Code: A set of research ethical principles that came as a result of the 1947 Nuremburg Trials at the end of World War II. Written because of the Nazi medical experiments, they are still used in many parts of the world.

O

Obedience to authority experiments: Studies that consider how people respond to being told what to do by a person who they think has power or authority.

Objective: A statement of intended outcomes to achieve goals of an intervention or program. They are ideally focused, time framed, and measurable, with some projection of when they will be actually achieved. They are typically used in program evaluation studies.

Objectivity: A presumed lack of bias or prejudice. In social science, it should be declared and verified only when it is checkable.

Observation: Using one's human senses to obtain information about something. It typically involves systematically recording an event, person, behavior, or phenomenon.

Observational data: Data obtained through direct firsthand observation by the researcher.

Observational study: A study in which the researchers do not seek to intervene; they simply observe the course of events. Changes or differences in one characteristic (e.g., whether people received the intervention of interest) are studied in relation to changes or differences in another characteristic (e.g., whether they died) without any action by the investigator.

Observed frequencies: The statistical occurrence of variable scores or values. This is usually used in contrast to expected frequencies, which are how often one would expect something to occur, given previous data, trends, or observations.

Observer: A person who watches but does not participate in what is being studied.

Observer bias, threat: The possibility that an observer does not observe phenomena objectively or accurately, thus producing suspect or invalid observations. This is deemed a threat to the internal validity of a study.

Observer–participant: A researcher who actually takes part in what he or she is researching, such as someone researching support groups and learning about them while participating in one. This is also referred to as a *participant–observer*. The technique is used frequently in qualitative research studies.

Observer reliability: Ability of an observer or many observers to consistently measure things the same way repeatedly. If this occurs across observers with the same conclusion of the observation, then it is referred to as *interrater reliability*.

Obtrusive data collection, threat: Gathering information in a way that causes difficulty or distress for participants. This may be deemed a threat to the internal validity of a study.

Odds: A ratio of the number of people experiencing an event to the number of people who don't experience that event.

Odds ratio (OR): The ratio of the odds of having the target disorder in the experimental group relative to the odds in favor of having the target disorder in the comparison or control group (in cohort studies or systematic reviews). It is also the odds in favor of being exposed to participants with the target disorder divided by the odds in favor of being exposed to control participants (without the target disorder).

Omnibus survey: A method in which information on a wide range of participants is collected during the same interview, for example, a consumer marketing survey of many products and their uses.

On-task behavior: When a person is engaged in or working on a specific task or activity in a study.

One-group posttest-only design: A preexperimental design involving one group that is given a test after treatment is given. It attempts, therefore, to evaluate a program's outcomes when no available comparison group and no pretest data are available (or needed, as in a client satisfaction study).

One-group pretest-posttest design: A preexperimental design involving one group that is pretested, exposed to a form of treatment, and then posttested.

One-shot case study design: See *one-group posttest-only design*.

One-tailed hypothesis: A statement of the initial expectations of what will happen in an experiment that predicts one possible outcome. This is differentiated from a two-tailed hypothesis, in which a researcher states that the dependent variable might change in either one direction or another but does not specify which way.

One-tailed test of statistical significance: The use of only one tail of the sampling distribution of a statistic when a directional hypothesis is stated, for example, a one-tailed *t*-test.

Online survey: A collection of structured questions and responses that are distributed by e-mail or over the Internet more broadly. A frequently used tool is a software program called Survey Monkey.

Ontology: The nature of reality and how one views and interprets that reality. This is often an assumption that underpines a research study of methodological approach.

Open-ended question: A question giving the responder complete freedom for any response; for example, "What do you like about research?"

Operating costs: Costs associated with items that contribute to the operation of a program. They are typically used in program evaluation studies.

Operational definition: Defining a term by stating the actions, processes, parameters, or operations used to materially measure or identify examples of it.

Operationalization of variables: Defining the parts of a study in concrete and usually numerical ways so that one can consistently know what one is studying. For instance, if depression is a variable, this might be operationally defined as participant scores on a validated measure of depression. This is important for replicating a study as well, allowing people to define the variable in the same way that the original researchers did.

Operations research: Mathematical, economic, or scientific analysis of a process or operation used in making decisions. It is often used for the analysis of problems in business and industry involving the construction of models and the application of linear programming, critical path analysis, and other quantitative techniques.

Opinion question: A question a researcher asks to find out what people think about a topic.

Opportunity costs: The cost that is equivalent to the next-best economic activity that would be forgone if a project or program proceeds. They are typically used in program evaluation studies.

Oral history: The recording, preservation, and interpretation of historical accounts and information based on the personal experiences and opinions of the participant. This can be gathered through interviews, poems, music, accounts of events, the study of myths, and so on.

Ordinal measurement: Assigning numbers to objects representing their rank ordering (first, second, third, etc.) of the entities measured. This is the second level of measurement, one up from the first, nominal level.

Ordinal scale: A measurement scale that ranks or orders individuals in terms of the degree to which they possess a characteristic of interest on which they can be ranked, for example, A students versus B students versus C students.

Ordinal variable: See *ordinal scale.*

Ordinary least squares (OLS): An estimation technique for statistical regression analysis. Estimates are used to analyze both experimental and observational data.

Original data: The raw data from an experiment that has or has not been analyzed. It is often referred to as the *raw data* or *existing data set.*

Outcome evaluation: Researching to measure practice or program effectiveness. Such studies examine what has changed as a result of the intervention being offered.

Outcome measures: Specific standardized or nonstandardized benchmarks used to assess whether the intervention or program resulted in any changes.

Outcome variable: See *dependent variable* or *criterion variable.*

Outlier, statistical: An observation in a data set that is far removed in value from the others in the set. It is an unusually large or unusually small value compared with the others. It might be the result of an error in measurement, in which case it will distort the interpretation of the data, having undue influence on many summary statistics, for example, the mean. All outliers should be scrutinized before data analysis.

Outside observer: A person other than the principal researcher who is often invited to repeat the measures completed by the researcher to guard against researcher bias.

Outsider-within: A social group's placement in specific, historical context of race, gender, and class inequality that might influence its point of view on the world.

Overgeneralization: Assuming that something will occur in the same way as it did before without really establishing a pattern, for instance, flipping a coin, and when it lands on heads, assuming it will do the same the next time. In reality, however, it is a 50-50 chance for each independent coin toss.

Overview: See *systematic review*.

P

Panel group: A group of persons who provide information or feedback to the researchers at different points of study. It is typically used in program evaluation studies.

Paradigm: This is the way a person sees and interprets the world according to a particular belief system.

Parallel-forms reliability: The degree of similarity attained by putting together two tests with the same content and running them both at the same time to see if they measure things the same way. This is a test that standardizes a measuring instrument.

Parameter: A numerical index describing a characteristic of a population, for example, its variance, standard deviation, and so on.

Parametric statistical test technique: A test of significance, appropriate when the data represent an interval or ratio scale of measurement and when other specific assumptions have been met, specifically that the sample statistics relate to the population parameters, that the variance of the sample relates to the variance of the population, and that the population has normality.

Parsimony: A philosophical principle preferring simplicity and succinctness in explanations. It is commonly stated as: "the simplest adequate explanation is usually the more correct one."

Partial correlation: A method of controlling the participant characteristic threat in correlational research by statistically holding one or more variables constant and then analyzing the data.

Participant: An individual or subject who is studied in research, often but not necessarily a student, patient, or client.

Participant observations: Observations in which the researcher actually becomes a participant in the situation to be observed. This is one of the main methods of qualitative research. See *observer–participant*.

Participant reality: However correct or biased, the way that a person actually sees or perceives the world. This is in contrast to objective reality, which is a concrete reality that would be available for everyone to observe and check.

Participant selection bias, threat: The possibility that characteristics of the participants selected in a study may account for observed relationships, not the independent–dependent variables.

Participants, research: Any subjects of a study.

Participatory action research (PAR): A form of inquiry focusing on the effects of the researcher's direct actions of practice within a participatory community, with the goal of improving the performance quality of the community or an area of concern. It involves all relevant parties examining together current action (which they experience as problematic) in order to seek change and improve it. They do this by critically reflecting on the historical, political, cultural, economic, geographic, and other contexts in trying to understand the issues needing change, followed by action steps.

Participatory evaluation: An evaluation model organized as a team project in which the evaluator and representatives of one or more stakeholder groups work collaboratively in developing the evaluation plan, conducting the evaluation, or disseminating and using the results.

Path analysis: A type of data analysis investigating linear and causal connections among correlated variables. It seeks to determine which variables influence others and in which ways.

Pearson correlation (*r*): A common index of correlation appropriate when the data represent either interval level or ratio scales. It takes into account each and every pair of scores and produces a coefficient between 0.00 and ±1.00. A positive *r* indicates that, as one variable goes up or down, so does the other. Negative or inverse *r* indicates that, as one goes up, the other goes down.

Peer review: Offering research methods, studies, or scholarly work to scientific scrutiny and critique by selected other experts in a respective field of study.

Percentage distribution: An actual frequency distribution in which the individual class frequencies are expressed as a percentage of the total frequency, equated to 100%.

Percentile rank: An index of relative position indicating the percentage of scores that fall at or below a given score.

Performance appraisal: A specific method by which employees are evaluated.

Performance management: Organizational management that relies on evidence about policy and program accomplishments to link strategic priorities to outcomes and make decisions about current and future directions.

Performance measures: The process of designing and implementing quantitative and qualitative measures of program results, including outputs and outcomes.

Periodical: A magazine, newspaper, journal, or other type of written work that is published in a chronological series.

Personal experiences, participant observations: A set of research strategies that aim to gain a close and intimate familiarity with a given group of individuals (such as a religious, occupational, or subcultural group, or a particular community) and their practices through an intensive involvement with people in their natural environment, often, though not always, over an extended period of time. This is typically used in qualitative research studies.

Personal identification number (PIN): A number assigned to a participant to maintain anonymity when collecting or analyzing data.

Personal journal, notes: Taking case notes about a situation being studied.

Phenomenology: The study of reports of structures of consciousness, like thoughts as experienced from the first-person point of view. This is one of the main methods of qualitative research.

Philosophical assumptions: Beliefs that are inherent in research methodologies but that are not always explicit.

Pie chart: A circular graphic illustration of the breakdown of data into categories, usually using percentages representing spokes in a wheel or wedges.

Pilot study: A small-scale study administered before conducting an actual study. Its purpose is to reveal limitations in the research method or intervention to be amended to create a better study, or to demonstrate the potential usefulness of an intervention.

Placebo: An inactive treatment or procedure, literally meaning "I do nothing." The placebo effect (usually a positive or beneficial response) is attributable to the participant's or experimenter's expectation that the treatment will have an effect.

Placebo effect, threat: When something studied seems to have an effect even though it is given as a control. For instance, if college students were in a study where they thought they might be drinking alcohol and they felt drunk, even though it turned out that their drinks were nonalcoholic, this would be the placebo effect. This is a possible threat to the internal validity of a study.

Plausible rival hypothesis: An intervening, antecedent, or other independent variable shown by evidence or judgment to influence the relationship between either an independent and dependent variable or a program and its intended outcomes.

Point estimates: The use of sample data to calculate a single value (known as a statistic) that is to serve as a best guess for an unknown (fixed or random) population parameter.

Poisson distribution: A statistical distribution with known properties used as the basis for analyzing the number of occurrences of relatively rare events occurring over time.

Poll: A survey of the public or a sample to acquire information about participants, for example, political surveys before elections, census data, and so on.

Population: The total group to which the researcher would like the results of a study to be generalized. It includes all individuals with certain specified and identified, or universe, characteristics of a defined class of people, facts, or events.

Population generalizability: The extent to which the results obtained from sample data are generalizable to a larger group.

Positive correlation: A correlation in which, as one variable goes up or down, so does the other one. Its value ranges from 0 to 1.00.

Positive predictive value: The proportion of people with a positive test who have the target disorder.

Positively skewed distribution: A frequency distribution in which there are more extreme scores at the upper or higher end than at the lower end.

Positivistic research approach: The perspective that the tools used by science to study biological, physical, and other aspects of the natural world can be usefully applied to study human phenomena. Theological or metaphysical explanations are avoided in preference to naturalistic accounts.

Postmodernism: The theory that reacts against earlier modernist principles, by reintroducing traditional or classical elements of style or by carrying modernist styles or practices to extremes. It emphasizes the role of language, power relations, and motivation; in particular, it attacks the use of sharp classifications, for example, male versus female, straight versus gay, old versus young, white versus black, and so on. Whereas modernism was often associated with identity, unity, authority, and certainty, postmodernism is often associated with difference, separation, textuality, and skepticism.

Posttest: A test given after an intervention to determine if and how participants may have been affected by the intervention.

Posttest odds: The odds that the participant has the target disorder after the test is carried out, calculated as the pretest odds multiplied by the likelihood ratio.

Posttest-only control group design: A research design involving at least two groups or participants. One group receives a treatment, the other receives no treatment, placebo treatment, or an alternative treatment condition, and all groups are posttested. This design is a quasi-experiment if the groups are formed naturally. It is an experiment if the groups are formed using random assignment.

Posttest probability: The proportion of participants with that particular test result who have the target disorder, calculated as the posttest odds/[1 + posttest odds].

Power of a statistical test: The probability that the null hypothesis will be rejected when there is a difference in the populations. The greater the ability of a test to eliminate false hypotheses, the greater its relative power or its ability to avoid a Type II error.

Practical significance: A difference large enough to have some practical effect, contrasted with statistical significance, which may be so small as to have no practical consequences. It is sometimes referred to as *clinical significance*.

Practice evaluation: To assess the impact of a specific intervention on a target and outcome on a participant or participant group. It is conducted in partnership with participants and promotes ethical clinical practice.

Practitioner–researcher: A person or professional who conducts studies and also works in the field that he or she is researching at the same time. They often conduct empirical research about people they work with to direct and inform their practice.

Pragmatism: The belief that the significance of something is best understood in terms of its effects.

Prediction: The estimation of scores on one variable or event from information about one or more other variables or events.

Prediction equation: A mathematical equation used in a cause-and-effect study. For instance, 64% of adult individuals who take two aspirin will alleviate their headaches in 32 minutes.

Prediction study: An attempt to determine variables that are related to a dependent variable.

Predictive validity: The degree to which scores on an instrument predict characteristics of individuals in a future situation. This is a psychometric property of the instrument or scale.

Predictor variable(s): The variable(s) from which projections are made in a causal study. They are normally independent variables.

Preexperimental design: A research design that involves studying only a single group of participants, either post-treatment only, or pre- and posttreatment. No control or comparison groups are used.

Pretest instrumentation: This refers to pilot testing the measurement instrument with a sample not used in the research study in order to correct any problems that it may have.

Pretest odds: The odds that the participant has the target disorder before the test is carried out, calculated as pretest probability/[1 – pretest probability].

Pretest-posttest control group design: A research design that involves studying at least two groups. All groups are pretested, then only one group receives a specified treatment, while the other group(s) receive no treatment, placebo treatment, or alternative treatment. Both groups are then posttested. If the groups are created using random assignment, this is an experimental study. If the groups are formed naturally, it is a quasi-experimental study.

Pretest probability prevalence: The proportion of people with the target disorder in the population at risk at a specific time (point prevalence) or time interval (period prevalence).

Pretest sensitization, threat: The pretest modifies the participant so that he or she behaves differently than unpretested participants. This may be a threat to the external validity of a study's findings.

Pretest study: An assessment test given before an intervention to determine the level on which a research participant falls before the intervention takes place.

Pretest treatment interaction, threat: The possibility that participants may respond or react differently to a treatment because they have been pretested. This may be a threat to the internal validity of the findings of a study.

Prevalence rate: The number of cases of a disorder, whether new or previously exiting, observed in a specified period of time.

Prevalence study: A type of cross-sectional study that measures the proportion of a population having a particular condition or characteristic, for example, the number of people in a town with a particular disease or illness.

Primary data: Information collected firsthand by the researcher for the study, for example, through surveys, observations, tests, interviews, and so on.

Primary research: The collection of data that does not already exist.

Primary sampling units (PSUs): A cohort or subgroup of the sample selected from the sampling frame in order to conduct data analysis.

Primary source: Firsthand information, such as the testimony of an eyewitness, an original document, a relic, or a description of a study written by the person who conducted it.

Privacy: The ethical imperative for research participants to have their personal information protected. This is required by federal law when conducting research on human participants.

Probability: The relative frequency with which a particular event occurs among all events of interest.

Probability Proportionate to Size (PPS) sampling: A sampling technique where the probability that a particular sampling unit will be chosen in the sample is proportional to some known variable, such as population size or geographic size.

Probe question: A question asked during an interview to trigger answers and certain responses.

Problem statement: A statement that indicates the specific purpose of the research, its questions or hypotheses, the variables of interest to the researcher, and any specific relationships between those variables that is to be, or was, investigated. It usually also includes a description of the background and rationale (justification) for the study. Well-written research includes these at the very onset of the study.

Procedures: A detailed description by the researcher of what was (or will be) done in carrying out a study or administering study or research protocols.

Process evaluation: This is called a level one evaluation, typically required for evaluation and demonstration projects, conducted to understand what was learned during the implementation of the project. These evaluations seek to answer what happened to whom and how in the program. They inform others about what they might expect if they were to launch a similar project. They typically include program descriptions, program monitoring, and quality assurance. They are typically used in program evaluation studies.

Process recording: A method in which interview content is recorded by creating a typed or written record of all communication both verbal and nonverbal, in addition to a record of the participant's and researcher's feelings and reflections throughout the interview.

Professional culture: A specific collection of values and norms shared by people and groups in organizations that control the way they interact with each other and with other stakeholders outside the organization.

Professional journal: An academic periodical that presents in-depth, original research in a specific field. Its articles have been peer reviewed by other scholars in the field for scientific standards and validity. Professional journals may also contain professional or industry-related news, updates, or book reviews.

Professional judgment: The mechanism used to decide how to act in a work environment. Normally, these are expert collective opinions of persons trained in specific fields or disciplines.

Program: A large or small defined intervention or purposive activity intended to achieve specific goals with particular target populations of individuals.

Program activity: An intervention or the work done in any program that produces outputs and outcomes. It is typically used in program evaluation studies.

Program drift: When a program or its goals, interventions, or processes deviate over time from their original intent.

Program evaluation: This assesses the impact of specific programs on individuals by determining their goals, objectives, activities, outputs, and outcomes.

Program implementation: This is the process of converting program inputs into specific activities needed to produce outputs. It is typically used in program evaluation studies.

Program input: Any resource used by the program's activities to produce outputs. It is typically used in program evaluation studies.

Program objective: This is a statement of intended outcomes of programs, written so that they specify the target group, the size and direction of expected change, and the time frame for achieving results, written in a measurable form. It is typically used in program evaluation studies.

Program outcome: This is the result that occurs in a program, that which it is designed to achieve. It is typically used in program evaluation studies.

Program output: This is a targeted goal of the program that shows its effectiveness. It is achieved by the program activities and is typically used in program evaluation studies.

Program process: An activity offered at any phase of a program that produces program outputs. It is typically used in program evaluation studies.

Program rationale: This is the reason why the program or intervention was implemented or funded. It typically aligns itself with the priorities of the particular governing or funding body that sponsored it. It is typically used in program evaluation studies.

Projective device: An instrument that includes vague stimuli that participants are asked to interpret. There are no correct answers or replies. For instance, in the famous Rorschach test, participants are asked to say what the inkblot picture shown to them seems to resemble.

Promising practices: This is a new strengths-based term applied to best practices.

Prompt question: A specific question used by a researcher to obtain a particular response from a participant during an interview. Prompt questions help keep the interview on track. Sometimes called *cued questions,* they are used frequently in qualitative studies.

Proofing research reports: Editing and amending the various documents assembled as a research document.

Proportionate sampling: A technique of sampling from a population that uses a sampling fraction in each of the strata (smaller population or group), which is proportional to that of the total population.

Proposal: A detailed, short description of a proposed research study designed and formatted in a specific way to investigate a given problem.

Prospective research: A research strategy that follows people forward in time to examine the relationship between one set of variables and later occurrences; for example, a researcher can identify risk factors for diseases that develop at a later point in time.

Protocol: A plan or set of defined procedural steps to be followed in a study. This enhances uniformity of studies, methods, processes, or interventions.

Proximal similarity: The degree of similarity between the elements of a study and the external elements, where the researcher plans to apply the results of a study.

Pseudoscience: A belief, practice, or methodology that resembles science but lacks proper credibility, checkability, methodology, or supporting evidence.

Psychometric properties, instruments: The two key traditional concepts in classical test theory are reliability and validity. A reliable measure assesses something consistently, while a valid measure targets what it is supposed to measure. A reliable measure may be consistent without necessarily being valid; for example, a broken ruler may undermeasure a quantity by the same amount each time (consistently), but the resulting quantity is still wrong or invalid.

Publication: A written work that is reviewed by a scientific peer review panel, printed, and distributed to the public. Publications may range from professional newsletters, to technical reports, to scientific journals, and so on.

Publication bias: A tendency, on average, to produce results that appear significant because negative or near neutral results are not published as frequently.

Pure research study: A study conducted without any intended practical end, which instead is conducted to explore an idea or to create a theory. It functions to advance knowledge and generate new ideas.

Purpose of a study: A specific statement by a researcher of what he or she intends to accomplish. It can be specified as an explicit statement, research question, study hypothesis, or study objective.

Purposive sample: A nonrandom sample strategically selected by the researcher because prior knowledge suggests it is representative or because those selected have the needed information. This is a nonprobability-based sample.

Q

Qualitative research: The systematic, firsthand observation of real-world phenomena. It has minimally three qualities: a focus on natural inquiry, reliance on the researcher as the instrument of data collection, and a report style focusing more on narrative data than on numbers; examples include ethnography, phenomenology, case studies, and so on.

Qualitative variable: A variable conceptualized and analyzed in qualitative studies. Typically, these variables have distinct categories, such as major or minor, and no real continuum is applied.

Quality assurance: A planned and systematic process that provides confidence in a product's or program's ability to serve its intended purpose. It is often used in evaluation research.

Quantification of variables: Measuring observations and experiences in numerical or empirical indicators, for example, 1 = female and 2 = male.

Quantitative data: Numerical data that either differ in amount or degree or are along a continuum from less to more.

Quantitative-descriptive design: To describe and quantify variables and relate them to each other so as to show to which variables impact others and why.

Quantitative research: Research that systematically explores, describes, or tests variables in numerical or statistical form.

Quantitative variable: A variable that is conceptualized and analyzed in numerical or statistical form. These variables are formed by using the hierarchical measurement scale of nominal, ordinal, interval, and ratio.

Quartile: In descriptive statistics, a quartile is any of the three values that divide the sorted data set into four equal parts so that each part represents one fourth of the sampled population. The first quartile (designated Q_1) is the lower and cuts off the lowest 25% of data (the 25th percentile); the second quartile (Q_2), or the median, cuts the data set in half (the 50th percentile); and the third quartile (Q_3) cuts off the highest 25% of data or lowest 75% (the 75th percentile).

Quasi-experimental design: A type of research design in which the treatment and control or comparison groups are not created using random assignment procedures. It does involve the manipulation of an independent variable and the specification of a test hypothesis.

Question: An expression of inquiry that invites or calls for a reply. There are fixed choices, or closed-ended questions, such as, "Do you like milk, yes or no?" and open-ended questions, such as, "Tell me what you think about milk."

Questionnaire: A spoken, written, or printed form used in gathering information on some participant or participants, consisting of a set of questions that assesses a phenomenon for research purposes.

Quota sampling: When the selection of the group of participants to be studied is made by the interviewer, who has specified quotas to fill from specified subgroups of the population. It can be either a probability- or nonprobability-based sample.

R

Random assignment: The process of assigning individuals or groups randomly to different treatment conditions for research purposes. This technique is a defining feature of nomothetic experiments.

Random digit dialing: A method for selecting people for involvement in telephone-conducted surveys by generating telephone numbers at random.

Random error: Problems in data or measurement caused by unknown and unpredictable changes in the experiment or participants. Confidence intervals (*CIs*) and *p*-values allow for the existence of random error but not systematic errors (bias).

Random numbers table: A specific table of numbers that provides a scientific means for random selection or random assignment of participants to a research study. These are usually appended in statistics textbooks.

Random sample, simple: A sample selected in such a way that every member of the population has an equal chance of being selected.

Randomization, random allocation: A method analogous to tossing a coin to assign clients to treatment groups. The experimental treatment is assigned if the coin lands heads, and a conventional, control, or placebo treatment is given if the coin lands tails.

Randomized controlled trial (RCT): An outcome study wherein participants are randomly allocated to an experimental group or a control or comparison group and followed over time on the variables or outcomes of interest. RCTs are capable of high levels of internal validity.

Randomized cross-sectional survey design: Research that obtains data from a particular population at a single point in time by randomly sampling all members of that population.

Randomized one-group posttest-only design: A preexperimental design in which a randomly selected group of participants receives an intervention and then is tested afterward to determine their status; for example, a random selection of lawyers who completed a bar examination preparation class are assessed in terms of their overall pass rates.

Randomized study: A study in which group members are chosen from a list of possible participants in a way that ensures all members of the group have an equal chance of being selected.

Range (*Ra*): The difference between the highest and lowest scores in a distribution; a main measure of variability.

Rank-ordering: Creating a logical relationship between a set of items such that, for any two items, the first is ranked higher than, ranked lower than, or ranked equal to the second. By reducing detailed measures to a sequence of ordinal numbers, rankings make it possible to evaluate complex information according to defined criteria.

Rapport: A harmonious interpersonal connection between two people. This is often important in conducting individual or group interviews with research participants.

Rasch analysis: A method for constructing a linear system from observed counts and categorical responses, within which items and subjects can be measured unambiguously.

Rate: This refers to how fast or frequent an event occurs, usually expressed with respect to time; for example, the mortality rate might be the number of deaths per year per 100,000 people.

Ratio measurement: A level of measurement with fixed ratios between units and with an absolute zero that is meaningful. For instance, savings is a ratio measurement, as zero savings means no savings. This is the highest level of measurement on the four-level scale, above nominal, ordinal, and interval. All the properties of the three lower level scales are also in this highest level scale.

Ratio scale: The highest measurement scale that, in addition to being an interval scale, also has an absolute zero in the scale.

Ratio variable: A measurement where the difference between two values is meaningful and in which there is a clear definition of zero. When the variable equals 0, there is the absence of that variable. Variables such as savings, pounds lost, or height gained are ratio variables.

Rationale: A logical statement of the reasons for conducting the study or taking a particular research approach. The rationale for the study is normally expressed in its introduction subsection. It is sometimes called the *story behind the study.*

Raw data: Data not yet processed for meaningful research or statistical use.

Raw score: The actual true score attained by an individual on the items in a test, inventory, scale, or other instrument.

Reactive arrangement or effect, threat: A way of conducting a study that may affect what is being studied. The very act of data collection can affect the items on which the researcher wants to collect data. For example, participants may tend to improve their performance just because they know they are part of an experiment. This may be a threat to the internal validity of a study.

Reactivity, threat: See *reactive arrangement or effect, threat.*

Real benefits: These represent the program benefits viewed as net gains to participants, communities, neighborhoods, or society. They are typically used in program evaluation studies.

Reality: The state of things as they actually exist and can be observed. Individuals may hold differing views of the same reality.

Record-keeping system: A systematic way of writing down or compiling data from a research study.

Recording error: A problem in the way data is written down, collected, transcribed, or stored.

Recording of data: Audiotaping, videotaping, writing down, or storing information from a research study.

Recruitment of participants: Finding ethical ways to obtain voluntary involvement from people for participation in a research study, while safeguarding their rights to participate or not participate.

Recursive causal model: A causal model that specifies one-way causal relationships among variables, for example, smoking and lung cancer.

Reductionism: This refers to breaking down components into logical and simple units so they may be described and studied by researchers.

Referee, external: An expert in a field who reviews a research manuscript and decides whether it will be published in a book or an academic journal. The review is normally conducted by an editorial review panel consisting of the author's peers in the field and done through a blind review system.

Reference: A source used to write an article, chapter, research report, or book. In the research literature, references are usually written in a particular style. For social science research, the style is almost always that published by the American Psychological Association (APA).

Reflective journal writing: The process of writing thoughts and emotions to sort through experiences in ways that emphasize metacognition, or thinking about how one thinks and feels. Research participants may be asked to keep such journals in a particular study. Sometimes referred to as *reflexivity,* this process is often used as a qualitative research study technique.

Regimen: A treatment plan (usually medical) specifying the dosage, schedule, and duration of the treatment or intervention.

Regression analysis: A general statistical technique that analyzes the relationships between a dependent (criterion) variable and a set of independent (predictor) variables. It seeks to determine what predictor or set of predictors influence the dependent variables.

Regression line: The line of so-called best fit for a set of scores plotted on coordinate axes or on a scatterplot. Using this line shows how far scores vary from each other and also allows one to see a visual pattern of the scores on the x-y axes.

Regression, threat: The possibility that results are due to a tendency for groups, selected on the basis of extreme scores, to regress toward more average scores on subsequent measurements, regardless of the experimental treatment given. This may be a threat to the internal validity of the findings of a study.

Regression to the mean, threat: A statistical phenomenon that can make natural variation in repeated data look like real change. It happens when unusually large or small measurements tend to be followed by measurements that are closer to the mean. This may be a threat to the internal validity of the findings of a study.

Relationship question: A question that explores a participant's connections to other individuals.

Relative benefit increase (RBI): The proportional increase in rates of good outcomes between experimental (EER) and control participants (CER) in a trial, calculated as [EER – CER]/CER and accompanied by a 95% confidence interval (CI).

Relative risk increase (RRI): The proportional increase in rates of bad outcomes between experimental (EER) and control participants (CER) in a trial, calculated as [EER – CER]/CER and accompanied by a 95% confidence interval (CI).

Relative risk reduction (RRR): The proportional reduction in rates of bad outcomes between experimental (EER) and control participants (CER) in a trial, calculated as [EER – CER]/CER and accompanied by a 95% confidence interval (CI).

Relevance: The applicability of research to some real-world problem. The answer to the questions "So what?" and "Who can benefit from this study?" highlight the importance of this issue.

Reliability: The degree to which scores obtained by an instrument are repeated and consistent measures of whatever the scale, instrument, or inventory purports to measure. One assesses the reliability of an instrument, scale, or inventory to standardize the instrument and to scrutinize its psychometric properties.

Reliability coefficient: An index of the consistency of scores repeated using the same instrument. There are several methods of computing reliability coefficients depending on the type of consistency and characteristics of the instrument, for example, interrater reliability, split-half reliability, coefficient alpha, and so on.

Reliability measures: Systematic actions, such as taking several or multiple measurements on the same participants, intended to make sure that research measurements are being consistently reproduced.

Replacement sampling: A statistical term meaning that participants are chosen and then put back into the sample, so each unit is replaced before the next is sampled. This means that, ideally, one outcome does not affect the other outcomes. In a finite population, this distinction is important, although in an infinite population, it is not.

Replication: This refers to conducting a measurement, experiment, or study again; the second may be a repetition of the original study using different participants, or specified aspects of the study may be changed. If the study is repeated and produces the same findings, this enhances the validity and generalizability of the findings.

Representative sample: A group being studied who are measured to have demographic characteristics (e.g., sex, age, race, etc.) that match the population at large. For instance, if females make up 51% of a population, a representative sample would also have this percentage of females.

Representativeness: The extent to which a sample is identical, in all characteristics, to the intended population. One has to inspect the selected sample and compare it with the population to determine this feature, not just assume it mirrors the population.

Research: The systematic investigation of a phenomenon. It is the process of searching, investigating, and discovering facts by using the scientific method. All research studies include, minimally, a specified purpose, a rationale for study, a specified method, analysis of data, and a conclusion.

Research committee: A group of selected experts who guide a researcher's work. These can be a planning committee, steering committee, or thesis committee.

Research consumer: A person who reads and applies research. Consumers are expected to appraise research methods and findings for their relevance.

Research design: The way that a research project is conducted. The main question answered here is, "What happened during this study?" This is one part of its overall method.

Research findings: The results of a research study.

Research hypothesis: A prediction of study outcomes. It is often a statement of the expected relationship between two or more variables based on testable assumptions, written in a directional or plausible form.

Research method: The main approach that will be taken to conduct the study, such as exploratory, experimental, descriptive, case studies, quantitative, qualitative, mixed methods, and so on.

Research participant: A person who is a participant in a study.

Research problem: A question that the researcher seeks to answer or a situation that a researcher wants to find out more about through a research study. The research problem is usually specified in the introduction of the research report and is often part of the rationale for conducting the study.

Research process: The progression of a research project: identification of the research problem, conducting the literature review, designing the study, gathering and analyzing the data, and publishing the results. This term is synonymous with the scientific method, which formally and minimally includes a statement of problem, literature review, method, results and findings, conclusions, limitations, and implications.

Research proposal: A detailed, short-form description of a planned study designed to investigate a given topic of study.

Research question: A situation that a researcher wants to find out more about through a research study. This is also a form of specifying the statement of purpose.

Research report: The final write-up of how a study was conducted, including these main subsections: abstract, introduction, method, and findings.

Researcher bias, threat: When the investigator conducting the study affects the results through his or her own preconception of what the study will find. This may be a threat to the internal validity of a study.

Researcher–practitioner model: A phrase used in the helping professions to describe professionals who base their practice decisions on empirical data and evaluate the outcomes of their own practices.

Respondent: A participant who fills out a survey or otherwise provides information to a researcher to study.

Respondent bias, threat: A type of response bias that can affect the results of a statistical survey if respondents answer questions in the way they think the questioner wants them to answer, rather than according to their true beliefs. This is also called *subject expectancy*. This may be a threat to the internal validity of the findings of a study.

Respondent-driven sampling: A technique for obtaining a sample that combines snowball sampling, with a mathematical model that weights the sample to compensate for the fact that the sample was collected in a nonrandom way. This is a form of nonprobability-based sampling.

Response bias set, threat: A type of response bias, such as acquiescence response error or social desirability response, in which a respondent replies to items in a multiple-choice questionnaire by choosing or avoiding certain response categories for reasons related or unrelated to their content or meaning. This may be a threat to the internal validity of a study's findings.

Response category: One of the alternatives from which a study participant must select in responding to a closed question, for example, true or false.

Response rate: The number of participants solicited for information who actually provided data. Oftentimes, the response rate is less than the actual number of respondents selected for a variety of reasons.

Results-based management: A philosophy of management that emphasizes the importance of intentional program or organizational results in managing the organization, its programs, and its people. It is typically used in program evaluation studies.

Results of a study: The findings presented offer the analysis of the data collected and generally include tables and graphs when appropriate.

Retrospective: Looking back at events that have already taken place.

Retrospective interview: A form of interview technique in which the researcher tries to get a respondent to reconstruct past experiences, for example, "Share what it was like when you were a teenager." It is often used in qualitative research studies.

Risk ratio: The ratio of risk in the treated group (EER) to the risk in the control group (CER). This is used in randomized trials and cohort studies and is calculated as EER/CER. It is also called *relative risk*.

Rival hypothesis: This is an extraneous hypothesis that challenges the main independent–dependent variable relationship. For instance, score change in a study of student anxiety could be attributed to a student having a good night's sleep.

S

Sample: The selected subgroup of the population for the study.

Sample distribution: The actual distribution resulting from the collection of data. A major characteristic of a sample is that it contains a finite (countable) number of scores, the number of scores represented by the letter N. These numbers constitute a sample distribution.

Sample size: The actual number of people or units in the sample.

Sampling: The process of selecting a number of individuals (a sample) from a population scientifically in such a way that the individuals are typically representative of the larger group from which they were selected. These can be nonprobability- or probability-based samples.

Sampling bias: This is when either an intended or unintended disproportion of the sample is within the study.

It is intended when researchers try to include individuals with certain characteristics to ensure they are in the study. It is unintended when sometimes, by chance, individuals are selected who do not reflect the population as a whole. Researchers must inspect their samples after data collection to assess the extent of such bias.

Sampling distribution: The set of values that one would obtain if one drew an infinite number of random samples from a given population and calculated the statistic on each sample. In doing so, all samples must be of the same size (n).

Sampling error: Expected chance variation in sample statistics that occurs when successive samples are selected from a population.

Sampling frame: The defined population from which a group of participants have been selected. For instance, if a researcher was studying students at a university, a list of those who attended that university would serve as the population sampling frame.

Sampling interval: The distance in a list between individuals chosen when selecting participants (sampling) systematically; for example, for every fourth person who enters the library, four is the interval used for sample selection.

Sampling ratio: The proportion of individuals in the population selected for the group being studied (sample) in systematic sampling, for example, 25% of all persons who attend the tailgate at a football game.

Sampling strategy: This is how a sample is selected for research or evaluation purposes. Two main strategies are probability and nonprobability samples.

Saturation: A mode of research immersion in which a researcher completely surrounds himself or herself with the participant and subject matter. This is one of the main qualitative techniques used. It also refers to the stage in data collection when new information merely replicates previously obtained data.

Scale: A scheme, inventory, rating form, or device by which some property, attribute, or behavior may be universally measured.

Scatterplot: The arrangement of points determined by the cross-tabulation of scores on coordinate axes (x and y) on a graph and used to represent and illustrate the relationship between two quantitative variables.

Scientific method: A way of exploring questions that includes, minimally, the following principles: a driving curiosity, systematic observations, a systematic method, logical inquiry, and objectivity. These are referred to also as the *scientific tenets of research and evaluation.*

Scientism: The view that scientific methods are capable of providing answers to all possible areas of human affairs. Scientism is usually repudiated by most social and behavioral scientists in recognition that science has little to offer when issues pertain to values and ethical questions.

Scope: The range, from high to low, in which a variable can be expressed or measured. For instance, if one is assessing teeth brushing behavior in young adults in the United States, one would choose a sample of such young adults instead of the population at large, limiting the scope of the project.

Scores: Actual numbers or results of a test or study.

Screening question: An inquiry that helps the researcher to see if a participant is suitable for a study. For instance, if one is seeking only people aged 18 to 21, then asking about their age before the study is a screening question to include only those participants.

Search engine: An online program used to find information by sorting information from large databases, for example, ProQuest, Jestor, and Google.

Search phrase: A word or group of words used to try to find information on a particular participant either in text or in electronic media, for example, in a search engine.

Search term: A key word from an article that often is listed in the abstract or used when searching for information.

Second-level coding: In qualitative data analysis, this involves describing what first-level coding themes, categories, or ideas mean, producing detailed examples from the transcript to back up each interpretation. First-level coding is a combination of identifying meaning units, fitting them into larger themes or categories, and assigning codes to them. In second-level coding, then, these codes are further reorganized and modified or subgrouped for subthemes.

Secondary account: Using information that comments on an event rather than records of the event itself collected in formal ways (e.g., clinical files) and less formal ways (unpublished reports). This is one of the main qualitative techniques used.

Secondary analysis: Any systematic examination of an existing data set that presents interpretations, conclusions, or knowledge additional to, or different from, those presented in the first report on the data collection and its results.

Secondary data: Information that was initially collected and possibly processed by people other than the researcher conducting the study. Common sources of secondary data for social science include census reports, large surveys, or organizational records.

Secondary research: Studies conducted using information that was initially collected and possibly processed by people other than the researcher conducting the study, for example, a meta-analysis of a group of studies examining a particular intervention.

Secondary source: Information received from someone who was reporting on something firsthand, such as a description of historical events by someone not present when the event occurred.

Secondhand data: Information that is received, taken from someone who did not have any firsthand experience of an event.

Selection bias, threat: This occurs with differential selection of participants for comparison groups. Score differences, consequently, can be attributed to pretreatment differences among groups. This may be a threat to the internal validity of the findings of a study.

Selection-maturation interaction, threat: When participant-related variables (selection threat) and time-related variables (maturation) interact. This may be a threat to the internal validity of the findings of a study.

Selection-treatment interaction, threat: The possibility that some characteristic of the participants chosen for the study interacts with some aspect of the intervention being studied. This may be a threat to the external validity of a study's findings.

Self-administered interaction: A clinical tool that study participants use by themselves, rather than the data collection being overseen by a researcher. For instance, a study participant might be asked to watch a video and report in confidence about it.

Self-administered questionnaire: A survey or form with questions that participants are asked to fill out on their own without the oversight of the researcher.

Self-censorship: The tendency of a research participant to avoid speaking freely, out of fear, as there will be some consequence for doing so. This is especially significant in terms of studies that research behaviors such as drug use, which are illegal.

Self-interest: The tendency for people to act in ways that will be of benefit to themselves in a study.

Self-observer: A research participant who describes his or her own experiences and perspectives rather than being watched by someone else, like the researcher.

Self-report: Information provided to the researcher from a research participant, which the participant obtained by observing and describing his or her own experiences rather than having someone else, such as the researcher, describe the behaviors.

Semantic differential scale: A type of rating scale usually having five to seven points, from high to low, designed to measure the connotative meaning of objects, events, and concepts. The connotations are used to derive the attitude toward the given object, event, or concept and are rated by the participant.

Semistructured interview: When a research participant is asked a series of mainly open-ended or prompt questions that he or she is free to talk about at some length.

Sensitivity analysis: A process of calculating the benefits and costs using a range of possible discount rates to see what the maximum and minimum net present benefit is for a project, program, or policy. It is typically used in program evaluation studies.

Sensitivity, cultural: The ability of a researcher to be aware and respectful of possible cultural differences in the study and to adapt the design to them.

Sensory question: A specific question asked by a researcher to find out what a person has seen, heard, tasted, touched, smelled, or experienced through his or her own senses.

Serendipitous information: Data that a researcher learns by chance during the course of a study that ends up being helpful to the study, although the researcher had not known that it would be when the study was designed.

Setting: The actual physical place where a study takes place. A study could take place in a laboratory, or it could be *in situ,* or in the natural environment where whatever is being studied occurs.

Sharing knowledge: Disseminating, presenting, or publishing information or making databases available to other individuals and researchers so that research can build on other findings.

Sharing of findings: An ethical responsibility to offer information that has been learned from the scientific and practice community, usually in the form of an article or presentation so that the research can be verified, corroborated, refuted, or challenged by more studies to advance knowledge.

Side effect: Any positive or negative unintended result of an intervention. Side effects are most commonly associated with drug testing studies.

Sieving procedures: Specific, detailed actions taken to systematically sort through information for research purposes; for example, every case file with a violent episode could be selected from all cases at an agency.

Simple frequency distribution: The number of times that a score actually appears in a data set. This is often depicted on a chart, table, or graph.

Simple random sample: A sample drawn in such a way that every item in the population has an equal and independent chance of being selected.

Simulation: Research in which an artificial situation is created and participants are told what activities they are to engage in.

Single system research (SSR): A study conducted with one person, family, group, or system to explore the results of an intervention targeting specific outcomes. Typically repeated measures of client functioning are taken prior to intervention, during intervention, and perhaps after intervention is discontinued. These designs are a form of idiographic research—studies involving small numbers of participants—as opposed to nomothetic research, involving large numbers of participants. It is also known as *single-participant* or *N = 1 research*.

Skeptical curiosity: A state of mind in which a researcher thinks critically about claims made about reality but also continues to study research questions and to critique and examine new research as it becomes available.

Skewed distribution: A nonsymmetrical dispersion of scores in which there are more extreme scores at one end of the spectrum than the other (not a normal bell-shaped curve).

Skip pattern, questionnaire: Questionnaire logic designed to direct respondents to questions based on previous answers.

SnNout: When a sign, test, or symptom has a high Sensitivity, a Negative result can help rule out the diagnosis. For example, the sensitivity of a history of ankle swelling for diagnosing gout (accumulated uric acid) is 93%; therefore, if a person does not have a history of ankle swelling, it is highly unlikely that the person has gout.

Snowball sampling: Asking current research participants to ask other people whom they know to participate in a study so that what is at first a small group of participants becomes a larger one. This is a form of nonprobability-based sampling.

Social desirability: The tendency of people to answer questions in ways that are typically acceptable in a particular culture. This will generally take the form of overreporting good behavior and underreporting bad behavior.

Social service program: Organized work in health, education, and human service organizations intended to better the conditions of a community.

Socioeconomic status: A concept that implies a combination of at least two dimensions—social and economic. The economic dimension is often represented by money or wealth as reflected in employment income, home ownership, and other financial assets (e.g., pension plans, savings, property ownership). The social dimension incorporates education, occupational prestige, authority, and community standing. It is often a background and independent variable in studies that can be subgrouped for analysis.

Software program: A specific package that assists in data collection, analysis, reduction, or presentation of research studies.

Solomon four-group design: A research design that involves random assignment of participants to one of four groups. Two groups are pretested, two are not, one of the pretested groups and one of the unpretested groups receive the experimental treatment, and all four groups are posttested. This is considered an experimental design and is useful in controlling for the effects of testing.

Source of evidence: A place where information to support a claim comes from. For instance, one could use studies published in journal articles, testimony from experts, or information from newspapers to prove or disprove a point.

Specificity: The proportion of people without the target disorder who have a negative test. It is used to assist in assessing and selecting a diagnostic test, sign, or symptom.

Specificity of variables, threat: This refers to how well the intervention or condition being studied is defined. Researchers operationalize variables in specific ways in studies. Because these variables will be operationalized differently in the population (e.g., different times of day will be used, different materials will be used, different buildings will be used), it is impossible to be certain that the way variables in a single study are used can be generalized to other ecological situations (i.e., to other combinations of time, place, and materials). This may be a threat to the external validity of a study's findings.

Split-ballot design: A way of arranging a study in which the sample is randomly split up into two or more groups, and each group is confronted with different forms of the question. This makes it possible to compare the response distributions of the different requests across their forms and to assess their possible relative biases.

Split-half reliability: A technique or method of estimating the internal consistency of an instrument in which two equal sets of scores are obtained from the same test, either one set consisting of odd items and the other set consisting of even items or the top half of the test items versus the bottom half of the test items, and are correlated. This is a test that standardizes a measuring instrument.

Spoon-feeding: Asking a question in a deliberate way so that it implies a particular answer, for example, "You are not really angry—correct?"

Spot-check record: Information gathered and written down that documents what happened in a particular place at various points in time.

SpPin: When a sign, test, or symptom has a high *S*pecificity, a *P*ositive result rules *in* the diagnosis. For example, the specificity of a fluid wave for diagnosing gout (abdominal fluid) is 93%; therefore, if a person does have a fluid wave, it rules in the diagnosis of gout.

Spread, data: A descriptive statistic that is a measure of variability, it is the number of points between the highest and lowest scores in a study. It is also called the *range (Ra)*.

Spuriousness: Incorrectly claiming a defined relationship between two variables when the relationship is simply accidental.

Stability of scores: The extent to which scores are reliable and consistent or repeated over time.

Stakeholder: A person or organization who has a vested interest in a study.

Standard deviation (SD): The most stable measure of variability, it takes into account each and every score in a normal distribution. This descriptive statistic assesses how far individual scores vary in standard unit lengths from its midpoint of zero.

Standard error (SE): The standard deviation of the sampling distribution of a statistic. It is a measure of the variation in the sample statistic over all possible samples of the same size. It decreases as the sample size increases, resembling the population.

Standard error of a statistic (SES): The standard deviation of the sampling distribution of a statistic.

Standard error of estimate (SEE): An estimate of the size of the error to be expected in predicting a criterion score.

Standard error of measurement (SEM): An estimate of the size or magnitude of the error that one can expect in an individual's score.

Standard error of the difference (SED): The standard deviation of a distribution of differences between different sample means.

Standard error of the mean (SEM): The standard deviation of sample means, which indicates by how much these means can be expected to differ if other samples from the same population are used.

Standard score: A derived point score that expresses how far a given raw score is from the mean in terms of standard deviation units on the normal curve. They are typically expressed in the form of z-scores or T-scores.

Standardization of variables: Transforming the characteristic being studied to a comparable metric known unit, known mean, or known standard deviation. This is especially important if what is being studied is not clearly standardized, as temperature, for instance, would be. There are four usual ways of standardizing: P-standardization with percentile scores, Z-standardization with z-scores, T-scores, and D-standardization, which dichotomizes a variable.

Standardized measuring instruments: Statistically scrutinizing aspects of instruments, such as scales, that provide for uniform administration and scoring and generate normative data against which later results can be evaluated. The instrument is scrutinized as to how reliable and valid it is.

Standardized research procedure: A process that carefully specifies how a study is to be conducted.

Static-group comparison design: A quasi-experimental research design that involves at least two nonequivalent groups; one receives a treatment, and both are posttested.

Static-group pretest-posttest design: The same as the static-group comparison design, except that both groups are pretested.

Statistic: A numerical index describing a characteristic of a sample or used to analyze data, for example, mean, standard deviation, and so on.

Statistical analysis: Analyzing and scrutinizing collected data for the purposes of summarizing information to make it more usable and for making generalizations about a population based on a sample drawn from that population.

Statistical equating: See *statistical matching*.

Statistical matching: This is a means of equating groups using numerical prediction. This integrates data on an individual observation from one source with data on a different observation identified as the best matching or most similar record from a second source. The best match is determined by objective statistical criteria that can be checked or verified.

Statistical power analysis: A calculation of the probability that the test will reject a false null hypothesis (that it will not make a Type II error). As power increases, the chances of a Type II error decrease. This can be used to calculate the minimum sample size required to accept the outcome of a statistical test with a particular level of confidence.

Statistical regression, threat: See *regression, threat*.

Statistically significant: The conclusion that results are unlikely to have occurred due to sampling error or chance; it means that an observed correlation or difference probably exists in the population. Statistical significance is typically defined as being when the chance or probability (p) of the correlation occurring by chance is less than 5%, or $p < .05$.

Stereotyping: Making generalizations or assumptions about the characteristics of all members of a group based on an image or perception (often biased) of what all people in that group are like.

Stigmatized group: Marginalized people in society who normally have less power than others, often including racial or cultural minorities, the poor, people with some social stigma (like prisoners), people with disabilities or diseases, or any group of people who are looked down upon by a dominant culture.

Stratified random sampling: A process of selecting a sample in such a way that identified subgroups in the population are represented in the sample in the same proportions in which they exist in the population.

Structural Equation Modeling (SEM): A general statistical modeling technique used to establish relationships among variables, SEM may be used as a more powerful alternative to multiple regression, path analysis, factor analysis, time series analysis, and analysis of covariance. A key feature of SEM is that observed variables are understood to represent a small number of latent constructs, which cannot be directly measured but only inferred from the measured variables using observed, latent, dependent, and independent variables.

Structured interview: A formal type of interview in which the researcher asks, in order, a set of predetermined questions to collect data, for example, an assessment protocol for persons to receive case management services.

Structured observation: Systematic recording of information about an event in forms that create parameters for the observation, most often in a checklist or tally fashion.

Study end point: The primary or secondary outcome used to judge the effectiveness of a treatment.

Study locale, site: A place where research is actually conducted. This could be in a laboratory or *in situ*, in a natural setting, or in more than one setting.

Sufficient literature, search: The researcher investigates a topic through a minimum of three search engines or databases. Then, the researcher tracks down a number of relevant leads to appraise various published and unpublished sources and materials about a topic he or she is studying. This location and appraisal of information can be done within the researcher's own field (e.g., social work) and from related fields or discipline areas about the topic of interest (e.g., nursing, psychology, sociology, education).

Summary: A brief overview of a research project, for example, an abstract, synopsis, executive summary, and so on.

Summative evaluation: An assessment of a program or intervention done after it has been implemented. This technique provides information about the program's outcomes and its ability to do what it was designed to do. For example, did the program meet its specified goals, objectives, and outcomes? It is typical of program evaluation research.

Summative measuring instrument: A test used at the end of an intervention or program to judge the effectiveness of the intervention or program overall.

Support costs: Costs that accrue to a program or project due to the support services and facilities used. Measures of support costs are typically used in program evaluation studies.

Survey interview: Research, often conducted by mail, e-mail, or phone, in which large numbers of participants are asked questions, and their answers are compiled to create statistical results.

Survey questionnaire: A research tool given to participants, who answer questions and then return their answers to the researchers.

Survival analysis: Data analysis that measures time to an event, for example, death or next episode of disease.

Systematic bias, threat: Any generally unintentional prejudice or inclination arising from constraints, such as observer bias and selection bias. This affects the accuracy of research results. Systematic bias and errors are consistent and repeatable, in contrast to random bias. This may be a threat to the internal validity of a study.

Systematic error: Biases in measurement that lead to a situation where the mean of many separate measurements differs significantly from the actual value of the measured attribute.

Systematic random sampling: Regular sampling using a known interval that begins with a randomized start. For instance, an individual sampling frame of households is established, and households to be sampled are selected using a constant sampling step.

Systematic review: A review of a clearly formulated question that uses systematic and explicit methods to identify, select, and critically appraise relevant research and to collect and analyze data from the studies that are included in the review.

Systematic sampling: A selection procedure in which all sample elements are determined after the selection of the first element, as each element on a selected list is separated from the first element by a multiple of the selection interval. For example, every tenth element may be selected.

T

T-score: *T*-scores are directly related to *z*-scores. With *T*-scores, the mean of the raw score distribution is equated to 50, and the standard deviation is equated to 10. Therefore, a *z*-score of +1.00 would be equal to a *T*-score of 60. *T*-scores are expressed as whole numbers. Thus, a *z*-score of −3.00 is equal to a *T*-score of 20. The elimination of negative numbers encountered with the use of *z*-scores is an advantage of using them.

Table: An orderly arrangement of data, especially one in which the data are formatted in columns and rows in an essentially rectangular form.

Table of random numbers: An organized arrangement of numbers generated in an unpredictable, haphazard sequence. Tables of random numbers are used to create a random sample. A random number table is therefore also called a *random sample table*. Many introductory statistics texts have examples of these.

Tacit knowledge: Knowledge that is difficult to transfer to another person by means of writing it down or verbalizing it.

Tag word: A nonhierarchical key word or term assigned to a piece of information.

Tangible costs: Costs that can be easily expressed in dollar amounts. They are typically used in program evaluation studies.

Target behavior: An isolated way of acting, selected as the object for a conduct change intervention or program. Target behaviors are also deemed to be the specified outcomes of the intervention or program.

Target population: The population to which the researcher, ideally, would like to generalize results.

Target problem: The issue or outcome being addressed by an intervention.

Telemarketing: The use of the telephone as an interactive medium for promotion and sales.

Telephone survey: A method of conducting a survey that involves calling participants on the telephone and asking questions from a prepared questionnaire.

Test of significance: An inferential statistical test used to determine whether or not the obtained results for a sample are likely to represent the population, for example, Chi-square, *t*-test, *F*-test, ANOVA, and so on.

Test question: An inquiry that gathers information about what a test taker reports.

Test-retest reliability: A procedure for determining the extent to which scores from an instrument are reliable over time by correlating the scores from, minimally, two administrations of the same instrument to the same individuals. This is a test that standardizes a measuring instrument.

Testing effect, threat: The prior measurement of the dependent variable may affect the results obtained from subsequent measurements. This may be a threat to the internal validity of a study.

Testing potential: The ability of a phenomenon to be assessed or researched.

Thematic analysis: This categorizes ideas, words, phrases, and sentences to either major or minor themes from the data. This is used frequently in qualitative data analysis.

Thematic notes: Information written down from an interview about particular groups of ideas or themes from the interview.

Theme: A unifying, recurrent, or dominant idea or motif that can be identified from the data set.

Theoretical sampling: This is a data collection process directed by evolving propositions or constructs during the course of a qualitative research study.

Theory: A coherent group of general propositions used as principles to develop explanations for social and behavioral phenomena.

Threat to external validity: Something that decreases the likelihood that the conclusions in a study would hold for other persons in other places and at other times, or the study's generalizability.

Threat to internal validity: An alternative explanation for research results, that is, that an observed relationship is an artifact of another variable.

Time considerations: Checklists and other ways of estimating how many minutes or hours will be needed to undertake the proposed research. These are normally mentioned in the method or procedure part of the study report.

Time effect, threat: A historical event at the time of a study that happens to all participants and alters the results.

Time order: A criterion for determining causality in addition to association. Time order means that the variation in the dependent variable occurred after the variation in the independent variable. Logically, any presumed cause must occur prior to any observed effect.

Time sequence: Pattern developed by the times at which the various episodes of a narrative take place. This is a way of tracking what happens chronologically in a study.

Time series design: A quasi-experimental design involving one group that is repeatedly measured, then exposed to an intervention, and repeatedly posttested.

Tradition: The handing down of statements, beliefs, legends, folklore, mores, customs, information, and so on, from generation to generation, especially by word of mouth or by practice.

Transcribing qualitative data: Taking audio recordings and writing them up to make manuscripts of the interviews. These verbatim write-ups are easier to use than the audio recordings when writing a qualitative research article.

Transcript: A written record of spoken language.

Transferability: A process performed by readers of research in which they note the specifics of the research situation and compare them with the specifics of an environment or situation with which they are familiar. If there are enough similarities between the two situations, readers may be able to infer that the results of the research would be the same or similar in their own situation. In other words, they transfer the results of a study to another context. This is related to generalizability but is a term more often used in qualitative research, which would have low generalizability but could have good transferability.

Transparency: Openness and accountability in research communication.

Treatment effects: Some research journals have achieved consensus on selected terms they use to describe both the good and bad effects of therapy. The following represent the main terms used in this regard: *experimental event rate* (EER) and *control event rate* (CER).

- *ABI (absolute benefit increase)*. The absolute arithmetic difference in rates of good outcomes between experimental and control participants in a trial, calculated as EER – CER and accompanied by a 95% confidence interval (CI).
- *ARI (absolute risk increase)*. The absolute arithmetic difference in rates of bad outcomes between experimental and control participants in a trial, calculated as EER – CER and accompanied by a 95% confidence interval (CI).
- *ARR (absolute risk reduction)*. The absolute arithmetic difference in rates of bad outcomes between experimental and control participants in a trial, calculated as EER – CER and accompanied by a 95% confidence interval (CI).
- *NNH (number needed to harm)*. The number of participants who, if they received the experimental treatment, would result in one additional participant being harmed

compared with participants who received the control treatment, calculated as 1/ARI and accompanied by a 95% confidence interval (CI).

- *NNT (number needed to treat).* The number of participants who need to be treated to achieve one additional good outcome, calculated as 1/ARR and accompanied by a 95% confidence interval (CI).
- *RBI (relative benefit increase).* The proportional increase in rates of good outcomes between experimental and control participants in a trial, calculated as [EER − CER]/CER and accompanied by a 95% confidence interval (CI).
- *RRI (relative risk increase).* The proportional increase in rates of bad outcomes between experimental and control participants in a trial, calculated as [EER − CER]/CER and accompanied by a 95% confidence interval (CI).
- RRR (relative risk reduction). The proportional reduction in rates of bad outcomes between experimental and control participants in a trial, calculated as [EER − CER]/CER and accompanied by a 95% confidence interval (CI).

Treatment fidelity: Specific checks placed in a study to confirm that the manipulation of the independent variable occurred as planned. It includes things such as treatment definitions specified, implementer training, treatment manuals written, supervision of treatment agents, sampling for consistency, proper utilization of data collection strategies, and so on.

Treatment group: Persons in the study who receive the independent variable that is being assessed to see if it makes a difference with these participants.

Treatment intervention: Planned care provided to improve a situation. Research explores the effectiveness of these interventions.

Treatment trial: This refers to a clinical trial that tests new interventions.

Treatment variable: The factor or condition that is manipulated (systematically altered) in an intervention study by the researcher. The main treatment is usually described by the letter X.

Trend study: A longitudinal design in survey research in which the same population (conceptually but not literally) is studied over time by taking repeated samples.

Triad: Nonquantifiable method of questioning three people simultaneously to understand why behaviors and opinions are as they are.

Triangulation: A technique often used to establish credibility in qualitative social research. It involves using more than two perspectives to determine the accuracy of some aspect of the study. It typically refers to concurrently using multiple data sources, data raters, or other research methods.

Truncation statistics: To shorten a number by dropping one or more digits after the decimal point.

Trustworthiness, qualitative research: The reliability and validity of qualitative research is conceptualized as: (1) descriptive validity, which refers to the factual accuracy of the account as reported by the qualitative researcher; (2) interpretive validity, which is obtained to the degree that the participants' viewpoints, thoughts, intentions, and experiences are accurately understood and reported by the qualitative researcher; and (3) theoretical validity, which is obtained to the degree that a theory or theoretical explanation developed from a research study fits the data and is, therefore, credible and defensible.

Tuskegee syphilis study: A landmark clinical study conducted between 1932 and 1972 in Tuskegee, Alabama, by the U.S.

Public Health Service. The participants in the study were not treated for their syphilis even though an effective treatment was available. This is arguably the most infamous unethical biomedical research study conducted in U.S. history and led to the 1979 *Belmont Report* and the establishment of the Office for Human Research Protections (OHRP). It also led to federal regulation requiring institutional review boards (IRBs) for protection of human participants in studies involving them.

Two-tailed test of statistical significance: Using both tails of a sampling distribution of a statistic when a nondirectional hypothesis is stated.

Type I error: A conclusion that a treatment or intervention works when it actually does not. The risk of a Type I error is often called *alpha*. In a statistical test, it describes the chance of rejecting the null hypothesis when it is in fact true. It is also called a *false positive*.

Type II error: A conclusion that there is no evidence a treatment works when it actually does work. The risk of a Type II error is often called *beta*. In a statistical test, it describes the chance of not rejecting the null hypothesis when it is in fact false. The risk of a Type II error decreases as the number of the participants in a study increases. It is also called a *false negative*.

U

Uncertainty: A situation where the current state of knowledge is such that: (1) the order or nature of things is unknown; (2) the consequences, extent, or magnitude of circumstances, conditions, or events is unpredictable; and (3) credible probabilities to possible outcomes cannot be assigned. Although too much uncertainty is undesirable, manageable uncertainty provides the freedom to make creative decisions. Some degree of uncertainty remains even in very carefully designed research studies.

Unit of analysis: The primary unit used in data reduction and analysis, for example, individuals, families, objects, groups, classrooms, organizations, communities, and so on.

Units of meaning: The smallest portion of an idea that can be regarded as a structural or functional whole.

Unobtrusive data collection: Measures that don't require the researcher to visibly intrude in the research context. For instance, an inconspicuous computer sensor hidden under a floor mat could record the amount of time that people spend at a museum display. Unobtrusive measurement should reduce the biases that result from the intrusion of the researcher or measurement instrument. However, unobtrusive measures reduce the degree the researcher has control over the type of data collected.

Unobtrusive measures: Measures obtained without participants being aware that they are being observed or measured or by examining inanimate objects (such as a school suspension list) that can be used in order to obtain desired information.

Unrepresentative sample, threat: When the sample does not represent or mirror the population. This usually results from an inability to randomly select the sample from the population to which a researcher wants to generalize. This is a threat to the external validity of a study's findings.

Unstructured interview: A series of questions presented by a researcher without any fixed set format but in which the interviewer may have some key questions formulated in advance. They allow for questions based on the interviewee's responses and proceed like a friendly, nonthreatening conversation.

Unstructured observation: A research technique in which the characteristics that will be observed are not predetermined. The researcher simply takes notes on the behaviors observed, as they arise.

V

Validity: The degree to which accurate inferences can be made based on results from an instrument. This depends not only on the instrument itself but also on the instrumentation process and how it is administered.

Validity coefficient: An index of the validity of two or more scores of instruments; a special application of the correlation coefficient (r).

Value: A belief of a person or social group in which they have an emotional and personal investment.

Value awareness: An understanding of how or what a researcher does, relating to and contributing to the overall purposes of an organization or program.

Value-for-money: An important goal for public officials and other stakeholders who are concerned with whether taxpayers and citizens are receiving efficient and effective programs and services for their tax dollars. It is typically used in program evaluation studies.

Value label: Putting a word to a numerical data entry point. This allows values of numeric and string variables to be associated with labels.

Variability: How spread out or closely clustered a set of data is.

Variability measures: How spread out a group of scores is. There are four frequently used descriptive statistics that are measures of variability: the range, interquartile range, variance, and standard deviation.

Variable: Any entity that can take on different values. Some values are numerical, but variables are not always quantitative or numerical. For instance, the variable *gender* consists of two text values: *male* and *female.*

Variable relationship study design: Such studies test the relationships between variables for determining how they impact, associate, predict, or influence each other.

Variable relationships: To test relationships between independent and dependent variables to determine how they influence each other.

Variance (SD^2): The square of the standard deviation and a main measure of variability.

Venn diagram: An illustration using circles to represent sets, with the position and overlap of the circles indicating the relationships between the sets.

Verification of the independent variable, threat: The extent to which one can reproduce the exact implementation of the independent variable. This may be a threat to the external validity of a study.

Videotape recording: A visual recording of events captured on videocassettes and played on a VCR. Videotaping has largely been replaced by recording onto DVDs or memory chips.

Visual aid: A presentation tool, such as a poster, PowerPoint, model, or video, that presents information visually.

Voluntariness: The ethical requirement that research participants are taking part in an experiment willingly without constraint or expectation of reward. Sometimes, small amounts of money or other forms of compensation are used to compensate for the participants' time, but these cannot be so valuable that a person feels involuntarily compelled to participant.

Voluntary consent: When a research participant agrees to participate through his or her own free will, without any force or undue pressure or influence. This is an ethical imperative when choosing research participants.

W

Weighting: Specification of the relative importance of items when combined.

White paper: An authoritative report, directive, or guide that addresses specific issues and how to resolve them. It is often used to educate readers and help inform a decision-making process.

Withdrawal design: A way of arranging a study that involves presentation and then subsequent removal of an independent variable.

Within-group research design: A type of experimental design where one looks at changes in outcome measures across treatments rather than comparing the changes with another (comparison) group.

Wording: The way that a question is phrased. Making questions and requests clear is important in research studies.

Working hypothesis: A proposition, or set of propositions, set forth as an explanation for the occurrence of some specified group of phenomena, either asserted merely as a provisional conjecture, or to guide investigation.

X

X-axis: The axis of a two-dimensional Cartesian coordinate graph that is usually drawn left to right (horizontally) and usually shows the range of values of an independent variable. It is also known as the *abscissa*.

Y

Y-axis: The vertical axis of a two-dimensional Cartesian coordinate graph that usually shows the frequency of occurrence of the variable being studied. It is also known as the *ordinate*.

Z

Z-score: A transformed score often called a *standard score*. The z-score for an item indicates how far and in what direction that item deviates from its distribution's mean, expressed in units of its distribution's standard deviation (*SD*). The mathematics of the z-score transformation are such that, if every item in a distribution is converted to its z-score, the transformed score will necessarily have a mean of 0 and an *SD* of 1.

CHAPTER 2

COMMONLY USED ACRONYMS, SYMBOLS, ABBREVIATIONS, AND TERMS FOUND IN RESEARCH AND EVALUATION STUDIES

Often, when you pick up a research or evaluation study or report to read or assess, the terms, abbreviations, symbols, or acronyms used within it are rather confusing. Researchers who write such reports need to be both technical and precise; however, they should be able to write their studies in much simpler ways than they do. The dissemination of important knowledge needs to be conveyed in ways that all consumers can understand (a main rationale for this glossary). The following is not a complete listing of such terms, just ones that pop up with high frequency in various research studies, reports, and journals.

FREQUENTLY USED TERMS IN RESEARCH AND EVALUATION STUDIES

ABI   Absolute benefit increase

ARI   Absolute risk increase

Answ.	Answer
APA	American Psychological Association
CATI	Computer-assisted telephone interviewing
CBA	Cost-benefit analysis
CEA	Cost-effectiveness analysis
CER	Control event rate
CoE	Code of ethics
DSM	*Diagnostic and Statistical Manual of Mental Disorders*
DV	Dependent variable
EBP	Evidence-based practice
EER	Experimental event rate
exp.	Experiment or experimental study
H	Hypothesis
H_a	Alternate hypothesis
H_0	Null hypothesis
HSO	Human service organization
ILL	Interlibrary loan
IRB	Institutional review board
IT	Information technology
IV	Independent variable
IVR	Interactive voice response
MIS	Management information system
NGO	Nongovernmental organization
NNH	Number needed to harm
NNT	Number needed to treat
NPO	Nonprofit organization
NS	Not statistically significant
O/B ratio	Odds-to-benefit ratio

OE	Observed effect or outcome variable (also known as DV)
PE	Program evaluation
PI	Principal investigator
PIN	Personal identification number
QL	Qualitative research
QN	Quantitative research
QoL	Quality of life
Ques.	Question
R or (R)	Randomization
RBI	Relative benefit increase
RCT	Randomized controlled trial
Rel.	Reliability
RRI	Relative risk increase
RRR	Relative risk reduction
S	Statistically significant
SSR	Single-system research
ToC	Table of contents
Val.	Validity
X	Main treatment effect (also known as IV)
X-axis	Horizontal line on a graph
Y-axis	Vertical line on a graph

COMMON STATISTICAL TERMS

α	Cronbach's alpha coefficient
ANCOVA	Analysis of covariance
ANOVA	Analysis of variance
ARIMA	Autoregressive integrated moving average
β	Probability of a Type II error or power of test

CFA	Confirmatory factor analysis
CI	Confidence interval
Crosstabs	Chi-square statistics
cum.f	Cumulative frequency
d	Cohen's measure of effect size
df	Degrees of freedom
EFA	Exploratory factor analysis
f	Frequency
F	*F*-test or Fisher's *F* ratio
HLM	Hierarchical linear modeling
K-S	Kolmogorav-Smirnov test
M	Mean
MANOVA	Multiple analysis of variance
Mdn	Median
Mo	Mode
MS	Mean square
n	Sample
N	Population
OLS	Ordinary least squares regression model
OR	Odds ratio
p < .05	Statistically significant
p > .05	Not statistically significant
P-value	The attained level of significance
ρ	Spearman's rank order correlation
r	Correlation coefficient
R^2	Regression
Ra	Range
S^2	Sample variance
SD	Standard deviation

SE	Standard error
SEM	Standard error of measurement
SEM	Structural equation modeling
SED	Standard error of the difference
t	Student's *t*-test
T	Standardized *T*-score
Type I	Type I error
Type II	Type II error
U	Mann-Whitney *U* test
Var	Variance, also *SD*^{2}
W+	Wilcoxon sign rank test
χ^2	Chi-square distribution
y	Dependent variable in regression analysis, or vertical axis in a graph
Z	Standard normal distribution
%	Percent
>	Greater than
<	Less than
=	Equal to
≠	Not equal to
≈	Approximately equal to
θ	Effect size
Σ	Sum
$\wedge$	Wilks's lambda

WEB TERMS

| **EBSCO*host*** | databases that provide premium online information resources for tens of thousands of institutions worldwide |

.edu	domain name for educational institutions
ERIC	the Education Resources Information Center, an online digital library of education research and information
.gov	domain name for government agencies
Jpeg	a commonly used format for storing compressed photographic images
JSTOR	archives of over one thousand leading academic journals across different disciplines
Mpeg	a standard for audio and video compression and transmission
.net	domain name for networking services
.org	domain name for nonprofit organizations
PsycINFO	abstract database that provides systematic coverage of psychological literature from the 1800s to the present
ProQuest	library archives of sources, such as newspapers, periodicals, dissertations, and aggregated databases of many types
PubMed	national library of medicine's Medline and pre-Medline database
URL	uniform resource locator, a website address
www	World Wide Web

FEDERAL GOVERNMENT GRANT AND FUNDING RESOURCE ACRONYMS

ACF	Administration of Children and Families
ACF-CCB	Administration of Children and Families—Child Care Bureau

AoA	Administration on Aging
ATF	Bureau of Alcohol, Tobacco, and Firearms
BJA	Bureau of Justice Assistance
CDBG	Community Development Block Grant
CDC	Centers for Disease Control
DHHS	Department of Health and Human Services
DJJ	Department of Juvenile Justice
DoA	Department of Agriculture
DoC	Department of Commerce
DoE	Department of Education
DoJ	Department of Justice
DoE	Department of Energy
DoL	Department of Labor
DoT	Department of Transportation
DoT	Department of the Treasury
EDA	Economic Development Administration
EPA	Environmental Protection Agency
FDA	Food and Drug Administration
FEMA	Federal Emergency Management Agency
G.R.E.A.T	Gang Resistance Education and Training
GSA	General Services Administration
HRSA	Health Resources and Service Administration
HSP	Head Start Program
HUD	Housing and Urban Development
IoP	Institute of Peace
JAIBG	Juvenile Accountability Incentive Block Grants
NCLB	No Child Left Behind

NIAA	National Institute on Alcohol Abuse and Alcoholism
NIC	National Institute of Corrections
NIDA	National Institute on Drug Abuse
NIH	National Institutes of Health
NIJ	National Institute of Justice
NSF	National Science Foundation
OJP	Office of Justice Programs
OMB	Office of Management and Budget
OMH-HHS	Office of Minority Health, Health and Human Services
SAMHSA	Substance Abuse & Mental Health Services Administration
SSA	Social Security Administration
TSA	Transportation Security Administration
VA	Veterans Administration
VAW	Violence Against Women

CHAPTER 3

COMMONLY USED STATISTICAL TERMS

There are many statistics used in social science research and evaluation. The two main areas of statistics are descriptive and inferential. The third class of statistics is design and experimental statistics. *Descriptive* statistics involve the tabulating, depicting, and describing of collections of data. These data may be either quantitative or qualitative. They provide a picture or description of the properties of data collected in order to summarize them into manageable form. *Inferential* statistics are a formalized body of techniques that infer the properties of a larger collection of data from the inspection of that collection. They build on these statistics as they infer the properties of samples to various populations. *Design and analysis* statistics were developed for the discovery and confirmation of causal relationships among variables in social science experiments. They use a variety of statistical tests related to aspects such as prediction and hypothesis testing. *Experimental analysis* is related to

As in the previous glossary chapter, if you are looking for a term and it is not here, please send it to my e-mail address, mholosko@uga.edu, with the subject line: "New Statistical Terms Needed." It will then be added in the next edition.

comparisons, variance, and ultimately testing whether variables are significant between each other. The latter two types of statistics are usually either parametric or nonparametric. The importance of statistics in the research process is sometimes exaggerated. Thus, a highly sophisticated statistical analysis rarely, if ever, compensates for a poorly conceived project, a poorly constructed research design, or an inaccurate data collection instrument. Thus, statistics certainly may aid the researcher but are never a substitute for good, sound thinking and attention to the scientific method and research process. For researchers, then, statistics are simply a tool to help them study the phenomena they are interested in.

DESCRIPTIVE STATISTICS

Measures of Central Tendency

Mean, arithmetic mean ($\overline{X}$ or M): The sum of the scores in a distribution divided by the number of scores in the distribution. It is the most commonly used measure of central tendency. It is often reported with its companion statistic, the standard deviation, which shows how far things vary from the average.

Median (*Mdn*): The midpoint or number in a distribution having 50% of the scores above it and 50% of the scores below it. If there are an odd number of scores, the median is the middle score.

Mode (*Mo*): The number that occurs most frequently in a distribution of scores or numbers. In some fields, notably education, sample data are often called scores, and the sample mode is known as the modal score.

Measures of Variability

Interquartile range (*IQR*): A measure of statistical dispersion being equal to the difference between the third and first quartiles. The first quartile (designated Q_1) is the lower and cuts off the lowest 25% of data (the 25th percentile); the second quartile (Q_2), or the median, cuts the data set in half (the 50th percentile); and the third quartile (Q_3) cuts off highest 25% of data, or the lowest 75% (the 75th percentile).

Range (*Ra*): The difference between the highest and lowest scores in a distribution; a measure of variability.

Standard deviation (*SD*): The most stable measure of variability, it takes into account each and every score in a normal distribution. This descriptive statistic assesses how far individual scores vary in standard unit lengths from its midpoint of 0. For all normal distributions, 95% of the area is within 1.96 standard deviations of the mean.

Variance (*SD²*): A measure of the dispersion of a set of data points around their mean value. It is a mathematical expectation of the average squared deviations from the mean.

Inferential Statistical Tests

Tests concerned with using selected sample data compared with population data in a variety of ways are called *inferential statistical tests*. There are two main bodies of these tests. The first and most frequently used are called *parametric statistical tests*. The second are called *nonparametric tests*. For each parametric test, there may be a comparable nonparametric test, sometimes even two or three.

Parametric tests are tests of significance appropriate when the data represent an interval or ratio scale of measurement and other specific assumptions have been met, specifically, that the sample statistics relate to the population parameters, that the variance of the sample relates to the variance of the population, that the population has normality, and that the data are statistically independent.

Nonparametric tests are statistical tests used when the data represent a nominal or ordinal level scale or when assumptions required for parametric tests cannot be met, specifically, small sample sizes, biased samples, an inability to determine the relationship between sample and population, and unequal variances between the sample and population. These are a class of tests that do not hold the assumptions of normality.

In the list of statistical terms below, when the test is a parametric test, the designation of *PT will be used at the end of the definition. Conversely, when the test is a nonparametric test, the designation of *NPT will be used at the end of the definition.

Statistical Terms

Alpha coefficient (α): See *Cronbach's alpha coefficient.*

Analysis of covariance (ANCOVA): A statistical technique for equating groups on one or more variables when testing for statistical significance using the *F*-test statistic. It adjusts scores on a dependent variable for initial differences on other variables, such as pretest performance or IQ. *PT

Analysis of variance (ANOVA): A statistical technique for determining the statistical significance of differences among means; it can be used with two or more groups and uses the *F*-test statistic. *PT

Autoregressive integrated moving average (ARIMA): This statistic is a Box-Jenkins approach to time series analysis. It tests for changes in the data patterns pre- and postintervention within the context of analyzing the outcomes of a time series design.

Binomial test: An exact test of the statistical significances of derivations from a theoretically expected distribution of observations into two categories. *NPT

Chi-square (χ^2): A nonparametric test of statistical significance appropriate when the data are in the form of frequency counts; it compares frequencies actually observed in a study with expected frequencies to see if they are significantly different. *NPT

Cochran's Q: Used to evaluate the relation between two variables that are measured on a nominal scale. One of the variables may even be dichotomous or consisting of only two possible values. *NPT

Coefficient of determination (r^2): The square of the correlation coefficient (r), it indicates the degree of relationship strength by potentially explained variance between two variables.

Cohen's d: A standardized way of measuring the effect size or difference by comparing two means by a simple math formula. It can be used to accompany the reporting of a *t*-test or ANOVA result and is often used in meta-analysis. The conventional benchmark scores for the magnitude of effect sizes are as follows: small, $d = 0.2$; medium, $d = 0.5$; large, $d = 0.8$. *NPT

Cohen's kappa (κ): A statistical measure of interrater agreement for qualitative (categorical) items. Scores range from -1.0 to 1.0. *NPT

Confidence interval (CI): Quantifies the uncertainty in measurement. It is usually reported as a 95% CI, which is the range of values within which it can be 95% certain that the true value for the whole population lies. For example, for a number needed to treat (NNT) of 10 with a 95% CI of 5 to 15, there would be 95% confidence that the true NNT value lies between 5 and 15.

Correlation coefficient (r): A decimal number between 0.00 and ±1.00 that indicates the degree to which two quantitative variables are related. The most common one used is the Pearson Product Moment correlation coefficient or just the Pearson coefficient.

Cronbach's alpha coefficient (α): A coefficient of consistency that measures how well a set of variables or items measures a single, unidimensional, latent construct in a scale or inventory. Alpha scores are conventionally interpreted as follows: high, ≥ 0.90; medium, 0.70 to 0.89; and low, 0.55 to 0.69.

Cumulative frequency distribution: A graphic depiction of how many times groups of scores appear in a sample.

Dependent t-test: A data analysis procedure that assesses whether the means of two related groups are statistically different from each other, for example, one group's mean score (time one) compared with the same group's mean score (time two). It is also called the *paired samples* t-test. *PT

Effect size (θ): Any measure of the strength of a relationship between two variables. Effect size statistics are used to assess comparisons between correlations, percentages, mean differences, probabilities, and so on.

Eta (η): An index that indicates the degree of a curvilinear relationship.

F-test (F): A parametric statistical test of the equality of the means of two or more samples. It compares the means and variances between and within groups over time. It is also called *analysis of variance (ANOVA)*. *PT

Factor analysis: A statistical method for reducing a set of variables to a smaller number of factors or basic components in a scale or instrument being analyzed. Two main forms are *exploratory (EFA)* and *confirmatory factor analysis (CFA)*. *PT

Fisher's exact test: A nonparametric statistical significance test used in the analysis of contingency tables where sample sizes are small. The test is useful for categorical data that result from classifying objects in two different ways; it is used to examine the significance of the association (contingency) between two kinds of classifications. *NPT

Friedman two-way analysis of variance: A nonparametric inferential statistic used to compare two or more groups by ranks that are not independent. *NPT

G^2: This is a more conservative goodness-of-fit statistic than the χ^2 and is used when comparing hierarchical models in a categorical contingency (two-by-two) table.

Independent *t*-test: A statistical procedure for comparing measurements of mean scores in two different groups or samples. It is also called the *independent samples* t-*test*. *PT

Kendall's tau (τ): A nonparametric statistic used to measure the degree of correspondence between two rankings and to assess the significance of the correspondence. *NPT

Kolmogorav-Smirnov (*K-S*) test: A nonparametric goodness-of-fit test used to decide if a sample comes from a population with a specific distribution. The test is based on the empirical distribution function (ECDF). *NPT

Kruskal-Wallis one-way analysis of variance: A nonparametric inferential statistic used to compare two or more independent groups for statistical significance of differences. *NPT

Mann-Whitney *U*-test (*U*): A nonparametric inferential statistic used to determine whether two uncorrelated groups differ significantly. *NPT

McNemar's test: A nonparametric method used on nominal data to determine whether the row and column marginal frequencies are equal. *NPT

Median test: A nonparametric test that tests the null hypothesis that the medians of the populations from which two samples are drawn are identical. *NPT

Multiple correlation (*R*): A numerical index describing the relationship between predicted and actual scores using multiple regression. The correlation between a criterion and the best combination of predictors.

Multivariate analysis of covariance (MANCOVA): An extension of ANOVA that incorporates two or more dependent variables in the same analysis. It is an extension of MANOVA where artificial dependent variables (DVs) are initially adjusted for differences in one or more covariates. It computes the multivariate *F* statistic. *PT

Multivariate analysis of variance (MANOVA): It is an ANOVA with several dependent variables. *PT

Newman-Keuls test: A type of *post hoc* or *a posteriori* multiple comparison test of data that makes precise comparisons of group means after ANOVA has rejected the null hypothesis. *NPT

One-way analysis of variance (ANOVA): An extension of the independent group *t*-test where you have more than two groups. It computes the difference in means both between and within groups and compares variability between groups and variables. Its parametric test statistic is the *F*-test. *PT

Pearson correlation coefficient (*r*): This is a measure of the correlation or linear relationship between two variables *x* and *y*, giving a value between +1 and –1 inclusive. It is widely used in the sciences as a measure of the strength of linear dependence between two variables. *PT

Pooled point estimate: An approximation of a point, usually a mean or variance, that combines information from two or more independent samples believed to have the same characteristics. It is used to assess the effects of treatment samples versus comparative samples.

***Post hoc* test:** A *post hoc* test (or *post hoc* comparison test) is used at the second stage of the analysis of variance (ANOVA) or multiple analyses of variance (MANOVA) if the null hypothesis is rejected.

Runs test: Where measurements are made according to some well-defined ordering, in either time or space. A frequent question is whether or not the average value of the measurement is different at different points in the sequence. This nonparametric test provides a means for this. *NPT

Siegel-Tukey test: A nonparametric test named after Sidney Siegel and John Tukey, which tests for differences in scale between two groups. Data measured must at least be ordinal. *NPT

Sign test: A test that can be used whenever an experiment is conducted to compare a treatment with a control on a number of matched pairs, provided the two treatments are assigned to the members of each pair at random. *NPT

Spearman's rank order correlation (ρ): A nonparametric test used to measure the relationship between two rank-ordered scales. Data are in ordinal form. *NPT

Standard error of the mean (*SEM*): An estimate of the amount by which an obtained mean may be expected to differ by chance from the true mean. It is an indication of how well the mean of a sample estimates the mean of a population.

Statistical power: The capability of a test to detect a significant effect or how often a correct interpretation can be reached about the effect if it were possible to repeat the test many times.

Student-Newman-Keuls (SNK) test: A nonparametric post-ANOVA test, also called a *post hoc* test. It is used to analyze the differences found after the performed *F*-test (ANOVA) is found to be significant, for example, to locate where differences truly occur between means. *NPT

Student *t*-test (*t*): Any statistical hypothesis test in which the test statistic follows a Student's *t* distribution if the null hypothesis is true, for example, a *t*-test for paired or independent samples. *PT

***t*-distribution:** A statistical distribution describing the means of samples taken from a population with an unknown variance.

T-score: A standard score derived from a *z*-score by multiplying the *z*-score by 10 and adding 50. It is useful in comparing various test scores to each other as it is a standard metric that reflects the cumulative frequency distribution of the raw scores.

***t*-test for correlated means:** A parametric test of statistical significance used to determine whether there is a statistically significant difference between the means of two matched, or nonindependent, samples. It is also used for pre–post comparisons. *PT

***t*-test for correlated proportions:** A parametric test of statistical significance used to determine whether there is a statistically significant difference between two proportions based on the same sample or otherwise nonindependent groups. *PT

***t*-test for independent means:** A parametric test of significance used to determine whether there is a statistically significant difference between the means of two independent samples. *PT

***t*-test for independent proportions:** A parametric test of statistical significance used to determine whether there is a statistically significant difference between two independent proportions. *PT

Tukey's test of significance: A single-step multiple comparison procedure and statistical test generally used in conjunction with an ANOVA to find which means are significantly different from one another. Named after John Tukey, it compares all possible pairs of means and is based on a studentized range distribution q (this distribution is similar to the distribution of t from the t-test).

Wald-Wolfowitz test: A nonparametric statistical test used to test the hypothesis that a series of numbers is random. It is also known as the runs test for randomness. *NPT

Wilcoxon sign rank test (W_+): A nonparametric statistical hypothesis test for the case of two related samples or repeated measurements on a single sample. It can be used as an alternative to the paired Student's t-test when the population cannot be assumed to be normally distributed. *NPT

Wilks's lambda (λ): A general test statistic used in multivariate tests of mean differences among more than two groups. It is the numeral index calculated when carrying out MANOVA or MANCOVA.

Z-score: A score expressed in units of standard deviations from the mean. It is also known as a *standard score*.

Z-test: A test of any of a number of hypotheses in inferential statistics that has validity if sample sizes are sufficiently large and the underlying data are normally distributed.

SECTION II

CHAPTER 4

SOME HELPFUL RESEARCH AND EVALUATION WEBSITES

In the final section, we offer you some field-tested, helpful research and evaluation websites that you can use to further understand research and evaluation concepts, terms, knowledge, and additional information. In Chapter 4, we present a range of quantitative, qualitative, evaluative, statistical, and additional research-related sites. In the final chapter, Chapter 5, we present the main or core journals in 13 schools and disciplines you may be studying or learning about and rank order the most significant respective journals in each of these fields.

A. QUANTITATIVE RESEARCH WEB RESOURCES

1. European Social Survey Education Net

This website was created by Norwegian Social Science Data Services and designed for those who are interested in using high-quality data from the European Social Survey to teach research methods. There are two main topics covered in this site: (1) an extensive online tutorial with exercises to complete involving the download of data sets and statistical analysis; and (2) a discussion forum and glossary are provided, as is a user guide, which will help beginners. The website also provides free NSDstat software for download.

http://essedunet.nsd.uib.no/

2. Web Center for Social Research Methods

Web Center for Social Research Methods is a website that provides a knowledge base and applied statistics for people involved in applied social research and evaluation. You'll find lots of resources and links to other locations on the web that deal in applied social research methods.

http://www.socialresearchmethods.net/

3. ESRC National Centre for Research Methods

The ESRC National Centre for Research Methods (NCRM) in the U.K. is a network of research groups, each conducting research and training in an area of social science research methods. It facilitates workshops and other activities in relation to a wide range of research techniques and offers educational research communities the opportunity to engage in capacities-building activities alongside colleagues from different disciplines. From this website, you can subscribe to receive information on developments and events in research methods, including a quarterly research methods e-newsletter and a monthly e-bulletin of forthcoming events, courses, training opportunities, and so on.

http://www.ncrm.ac.uk/

4. Sample Size Calculator

This site provides a sample size calculator that helps you determine an appropriate sample size given the population size, the sampling error, and the confidence interval you want. There are also links on the left-side menu to survey information and statistical significance.

http://www.surveysystem.com/sscalc.htm

5. The Survey Research Center—University of Michigan

The Survey Research Center (SRC) has been a national and international leader in interdisciplinary social science research involving the collection or analysis of data from scientific sample surveys. This site offers an introduction to various basic and applied empirical survey-based research that is theoretically informed. SRC seeks to bring empiricism to bear on problems that are of both social and scientific importance.

http://www.src.isr.umich.edu/projects.aspx

6. World Bank Group, Social Analysis

This website introduces social analysis work at the World Bank, including publications, training, and events. Links are also directed to various research tools and resources, including relevant research methods, when working within and with communities related to development. These cover analytical tools, participatory methods, and workshop-based methods as well as quantitative and qualitative research methods.

http://web.worldbank.org/WBSITE/EXTERNAL/TOPICS/
EXTSOCIALDEV/0,,menuPK:3177455~pagePK:64168427
~piPK:64168435~theSitePK:3177395,00.html

7. The Research Methods WWW Tutorial

This website, aimed at undergraduates, is designed to provide a basic introductory tutorial to research methods. Sections include research methods, variables and relationships, and common errors made in research. There is also a section demonstrating how to start a research project. The website offers extra materials that are not covered during class.

http://sociology.camden.rutgers.edu/jfm/tutorial/main.htm

8. European Association of Methodology

This website was created by the European Association of Methodology (EAM), founded in 2004 by members from a number of different European methodology groups. The EAM exists to promote empirical research methods in behavioral, social, educational, health, and economic sciences as well as in the field of evaluation. It is a membership organization, but the annual fee for students is comparatively low. For nonmembers, there are details about conferences, links to tables of contents of the association's journal, and the full text of statutes and minutes. The website focuses more on quantitative methods.

http://www.eam-online.org/

9. ThesisTools

This website allows readers to create free online questionnaires for use in research. It is helpful for a student at the stage of writing thesis to use quantitative methods in his or her research project. The free version runs for 3 months, and then there is an additional fee if one wishes to run the questionnaire for longer. The website also offers several forums where you can talk to other students and promote your questionnaire. ThesisTools asks users to send in a summary of research results in return for the use of the free survey. Some of the most recent summaries are published on the website.

http://www.thesistools.com/so/site/index.php?userID=&ln interface=eng&show

10. Social Sciences Data and Software Blog

The Social Sciences Data and Software Blog (SSDS) offers updated social science data resources, including the U.S. census, and provides information on how to select and use quantitative and qualitative analysis software. The website also includes links to many external social research resources, news, and event information.

http://www.stanford.edu/group/ssds/weblog/

11. American Statistical Association—Survey Research Methods Section

The Survey Research Methods Section (SRMS) website aims to improve practice and understanding by promoting research into survey methods. This site provides information about the SRMS, online issues of the proceedings of the SRMS, online brochures about survey research, and details of upcoming conferences and publications.

http://www.amstat.org/sections/SRMS/index.html

12. Henry A. Murray Research Archive

The Henry A. Murray Research Archive is part of the Institute for Quantitative Social Science at Harvard University and acts as a permanent repository for data (text, audio, and video). The website comprises hundreds of research studies with the aim to make these available for new research projects. The website provides detailed information on the data sets, supporting documentation, plus access or download arrangements for each data set.

http://www.murray.harvard.edu/

13. Introduction to Quantitative Methods

This is an online course in basic statistics. It was developed by Professor Gene V. Glass from the College of Education at Arizona State University, United States. This website provides a number of modules, each with some test questions at the end. It covers both descriptive and inferential methods, detailing the statistical tests that can be used, such as the *t*-test, ANOVA, and correlation. There is also a section of useful links to resources for statistics.

http://glass.ed.asu.edu/stats/

14. Center for Statistics and the Social Sciences

This website is based at the Center for Statistics and the Social Sciences (CSSS) at the University of Washington in Seattle. It offers information about social science statistics through working papers and seminars, seed grants to help initiate research projects, and overviews of courses they run. Links are also given to other relevant resources. The working papers are available online as PDF documents.

http://www.csss.washington.edu/

B. QUALITATIVE RESEARCH WEB RESOURCES

1. The Qualitative Research Consultants Association

This is a not-for-profit organization that promotes excellence in all aspects of qualitative research. From this site, you can get access to nearly 1,000 qualitative research consultants throughout the world. The research consultants include focus group moderators, facilitators, interviewers, and planners in many types of qualitative research.

http://www.qrca.org/

2. QualPage: Resources for Qualitative Research

This website has a broad range of online resources on qualitative research. There are also links to qualitative research organizations, discussion forums for qualitative research, and publishers of qualitative research journals, along with a listing of conferences that may be of interest to qualitative researchers. Additionally, the website offers a relatively comprehensive set of links to makers of qualitative data analysis software.

http://www.qualitativeresearch.uga.edu/QualPage/

3. Qualitative Research—School of Education, University of Colorado at Denver

This website provides online resources for the art of qualitative educational research: critiques, literature reviews, research design methodologies, and other articles. The resource is intended as an aid to educational practitioners as informed consumers of published research and as active contributors to the body of knowledge that informs emerging practices involving information and learning technologies (ILT).

http://carbon.ucdenver.edu/~mryder/itc_data/pract_res.html

4. Qualitative Research Software

This website provides qualitative research software (QSR) products that are different from statistical or quantitative software, which analyze data using numbers. QSR helps you to access, manage, shape, and analyze detailed textual, audio, and visual information.

http://www.qsrinternational.com/

5. Qualitative Research Webpage

This website was created by Dr. Don Ratcliff of Vanguard University of Southern California and contains notes and materials on a qualitative research course. It summarizes the qualitative–quantitative debate and the strengths, weaknesses, and approaches for each and discusses sampling and selection-related issues for qualitative data collection. The webpage also provides a list of links to further resources in qualitative research.

http://qualitativeresearch.ratcliffs.net/

6. Association for Qualitative Research (Australia)

This website aims to promote the practice and study of qualitative research. It is based at an association for qualitative research at La Trobe University in Australia and has been operating since 1997. The association runs a regular series of conferences, and the website details forthcoming and past conferences. Back issues of the association's qualitative research journal are available free available in PDF format.

http://www.latrobe.edu.au/aqr/

7. Association for Qualitative Research

This website is based at the Association for Qualitative Research (AQR) in the U.K. It promotes the professional interests of qualitative research among practitioners and field personnel. This site has information that would also be of interest to those engaged in academic qualitative research, including an overview of best practice methods for recruiting respondents for qualitative research projects, plus a range of articles and papers on qualitative research topics.

http://www.aqr.org.uk/

8. User-Friendly Handbook for Mixed Method Evaluations

This is a free online handbook guide to using a mixture of methods, that is, using both quantitative and qualitative techniques in research. The handbook was published by the National Science Foundation's Directorate for Education and Human Resources in 1997. It offers information on qualitative techniques and discusses how they can be combined effectively with quantitative measures.

http://www.nsf.gov/pubs/1997/nsf97153/start.htm

9. International Institute for Qualitative Methodology

This is the home page of the International Institute for Qualitative Methodology. The site is maintained by the institute from their headquarters at the University of Alberta in Edmonton, Alberta, Canada. The institute aims to foster progress in qualitative research and methodology and to enable dialogue between international researchers in this area. Information on publications, workshops, conferences, and research training is provided, alongside links to related resources.

http://www.uofaweb.ualberta.ca/iiqm/

10. PARnet

This website aims to create a self-monitored, community-managed knowledge base and gateway to action research resources, connecting practitioners and scholars with each other, the literature, and other educational opportunities. It is not affiliated with any particular institution but is currently maintained by the Cornell Participatory Action Research Network in the United States.

http://www.parnet.org/

11. Research Methods Knowledge Base

The Research Methods Knowledge Base is a free online textbook for an introductory course in social research methods. The knowledge base was created by William M. K.

Trochim, a professor in the Department of Policy Analysis and Management at Cornell University. It covers all aspects of the whole research process, including theoretical and practical topics. These include defining a research question, sampling, measurement, research design, and data analysis. The Research Methods Knowledge Base is also available as a printed book for purchase.

http://www.socialresearchmethods.net/kb/

12. Grounded Theory Institute

This site is concerned with the development of grounded theory. Details of seminars run by the Grounded Theory Institute are given, and there is also an online forum for questions and information. Nonmembers can access the general forum, but you have to join to see the other specific topic forums.

http://www.groundedtheory.org/

C. EVALUATION RESEARCH WEB RESOURCES

1. The Collaborative, Participatory, and Empowerment Evaluation, the American Evaluation Association

The Collaborative, Participatory, and Empowerment (CP&E) Evaluation is used throughout the world, including Australia, Brazil, Canada, Ethiopia, Finland, Israel, Japan, Mexico, Nepal, New Zealand, South Africa, Spain, the United Kingdom, and the United States. This webpage has a vast array of useful evaluation tools and information. It is an iterative, organic, and growing webpage.

http://homepage.mac.com/profdavidf/empowerment evaluation.htm

2. Resources for Methods in Evaluation and Social Research

This site lists resources for methods in evaluation and social research. The focus is on how to do evaluation research and the methods used: surveys, focus groups, sampling, interviews, and other methods. Most of these links are to resources that can be read over the web. A few, like the GAO books, are for books that can be ordered for free (if you live in the U.S.), as well as read over the web.

http://gsociology.icaap.org/methods/

3. Impact Evaluation: Methodological and Operational Issues, Asian Development Bank

This quick reference provides an overview of methods available for evaluating impacts of development programs and addresses some common operational concerns about their practical applications.

http://www.adb.org/Documents/Handbooks/Impact-Analysis/default.asp

4. Centers for Disease Control Evaluation Working Group

Use this website to learn about the Centers for Disease Control (CDC) Evaluation Working Group and its efforts to promote program evaluation in public health. The working group focuses on developing products and services in two areas: (1) defining and organizing the essential elements of program evaluation; and (2) leading institutional change to promote evaluation practice at the CDC and throughout the public health system.

http://www.cdc.gov/eval/resources.htm

5. The United Nations Evaluation Group

The United Nations Evaluation Group (UNEG) is a professional network that brings together the units responsible for evaluation in the UN system, including specialized agencies, funds, programs, and affiliated organizations. UNEG aims to strengthen the objectivity, effectiveness, and visibility of the evaluation function across the UN system and to advocate the importance of evaluation for learning, decision making, and accountability. There are a variety of web resources on evaluation research and publications.

http://www.uneval.org

6. Canadian Evaluation Society

There are extensive resources on evaluation through linked external resources. Links are from around the world and on many topics.

http://evaluationcanada.ca/site.cgi?s=6&ss=3

7. Evaluation Handbook

The purposes of this document are to (1) offer suggestions to reforming administrators in the how-to of a good evaluation, (2) alleviate some of the fear and mystery of evaluation, and (3) provide guidelines for evaluation.

http://www.ed.gov/about/offices/list/ope/fipse/biblio.html

8. InnoNet

Organized to enable public and nonprofit organizations to better plan, execute, and evaluate their service and agencies. They provide a search service for model programs, effective approaches to social services, and a participatory evaluation service. They have a workstation to help agencies develop strategic plans, program action plans, evaluation plans, program budgets, fund-raising plans, and grant applications. Their repair center helps organizations improve, create, and download surveys, interviews, focus groups, questionnaires, and data collection and analysis tools.

http://www.innonet.org

9. W.K. Kellogg Foundation Evaluation Handbook

This site presents a framework for thinking about evaluation as a relevant and useful program tool and outlines a blueprint for designing and conducting evaluations. Case studies of the Kellogg Foundation evaluations can be found.

http://www.wkkf.org/pubs/pub770.pdf

http://www.wkkf.org/programming/resourceoverview.aspx?CID=281&ID=770

10. Logic Model Development Guide

This guide was developed to provide practical assistance to nonprofits engaged in this process. In the pages of this guide, we hope to give nonprofit staffs and community members alike sufficient orientation to the underlying principles of logic modeling to use this tool to enhance their program planning, implementation, and dissemination activities.

http://www.wkkf.org/programming/reourceoverview.aspx?CID=281&ID=3669

11. Online Evaluation Resource Library

This website is composed of plans, instruments, and reports that have been used to conduct evaluations of projects. It also contains glossaries of evaluation terminology, criteria for best practices, and scenarios illustrating how evaluation resources can be used as is or adapted.

http://oerl.sri.com

12. Outcome Measurement in Nonprofit Organizations, Current Practices and Recommendations

This is a collaborative report by the Independent Sector and the Urban Institute.

http://www.independentsector.org/programs/research/outcomes.pdf

13. Outcome Measurement Initiative, United Way of Connecticut

Outcome measurement resources available on this website include forms and tools, support links by service areas, literature on the Outcome Management Press, orientation presentation, and more.

http://www.ctunitedway.org/what/outcomemeasurement.asp

14. Program Development and Evaluation, University of Wisconsin

Here, you'll find extensive resources and training links, including publications, workshops, and presentations; evaluation studies and instruments; and much more. There are practical, easy-to-use guides designed to help better plan and implement credible and useful evaluations.

http://www.uwex.edu/ces/pdande/evaluation/index.html

15. Untied Way Outcome Measurement Resource Network

The network purpose is to provide outcome measurement resources and instruction. Sections include updates with an automatic notification of changes, publications, current projects, and a resource library with articles, information, and research studies and reports.

http://national.unitedway.org/outcomes/

D. STATISTICAL RESEARCH
WEB RESOURCES

1. American Statistical Association—Survey Research Methods Section

The American Statistical Association (ASA) provides its members and the public with up-to-date, useful information about statistics. This site is the survey research methods section of the ASA. It aims to improve practice and understanding by promoting research into survey methods. The site includes information about the survey research methods, online issues of journals, and information about upcoming conferences and publications.

http://www.amstat.org/sections/SRMS/index.html

2. Statistical Society of Canada

This is the website of the Statistical Society of Canada. It has information on the development of statistical methodology and annual meetings, with detailed descriptions of research topics and data sets. There is a complete directory of members and details of regional associations and subgroups. This site is available in French and English.

http://www.ssc.ca/

3. United Nations Statistics Division: Social Indicators

This site is compiled by the United Nations Statistics Division (UNSD). It provides social indicators covering a wide range of subject matter fields from many national and international sources. The indicators include UN subject areas, such as population, childbirth, contraception, education, income, housing, health, literacy, unemployment, and sanitation. Statistics are available on webpages or to download as Excel files.

http://unstats.un.org/unsd/demographic/products/socind/

4. International Statistical Institute

The International Statistical Institute (ISI) is one of the oldest international scientific associations functioning in the modern world. The site contains information on the structure and activities of ISI and on its publications—particularly the *International Statistical Review* and *Statistical Theory and Method Abstracts*.

http://isi.cbs.nl/

5. Council of American Survey Research Organizations

The Council of American Survey Research Organizations (CASRO) is a professional membership organization that represents more than 300 companies and market research operations in the United States and abroad. The CASRO website includes the full text of their *Code of Standards and Ethics for Survey Research* and *Guidelines for Survey Research Quality*. Members have access to more resources, including surveys, standards, guidelines, proceedings, a newsletter archive, and an industry forum.

http://www.casro.org/

6. Council of European Social Science Data Archives

The Council of European Social Science Data Archives (CESSDA) is an umbrella organization for social science data archives across Europe. The website includes a clickable map to social science data archives around Europe and a common, integrated data catalogue. The site also includes links to the data archives' own websites and further information on CESSDA, including official documents and a list of seminars, as well as information on managing and accessing data.

http://www.cessda.org

7. University of California Los Angeles Statistics Preprints

The University of California Los Angeles (UCLA) statistics department provides more than 500 papers in their prepublication format. The papers are listed in numerical order of submission, and you can browse the complete list or a section of the list. The content of the papers reflects the research strengths of the UCLA Statistics Department: teaching of statistics, advanced linear models, descriptive multivariate analysis, survey construction, and analysis and structural equation modeling.

http://preprints.stat.ucla.edu/

8. Center for Statistics and the Social Sciences

The Center for Statistics and the Social Sciences promotes collaborative interdisciplinary research on statistical methods for the social sciences and teaches a rich menu of courses for social science students. This site offers information about social science statistics, including working papers and seminars. Links are also given to other relevant resources.

http://www.csss.washington.edu/

9. United States Census Bureau

This is the U.S. Census Bureau webpage. The Census Bureau serves as a leading source of data about America's people and economy. At this site, you will be able to locate public resources from the U.S. Census Bureau, including population, economic, industry, and geography studies. Data are available on webpages or to download as Excel files.

http://www.census.gov

10. Federal Statistical Sources

Federal Statistical Sources (FedStats) provides access to the full range of official statistical information produced by the federal government. This site offers data and trend information on topics such as economic and population trends, crime, education, health care, aviation safety, energy use, farm production, and more. Links are directed to both statistics and statistical agencies.

http://www.fedstats.gov/

11. InfoNation

InfoNation is an official United Nations (UN) database that is designed to allow members of the public to view current statistical data on member countries of the UN. This site allows you to compare statistics for up to six countries in up to five categories—economy, population, environment, technology, and health.

http://www.un.org/Pubs/CyberSchoolBus/infonation/e_infonation.htm

12. Population Index on the Web

Population Index is the primary reference tool for the world's population literature. This website covers all fields of interest to demographers, including fertility, mortality, population size and growth, migration, nuptiality and the family, research methodology, projections and predictions, historical demography, and demographic and economic interrelations.

http://popindex.princeton.edu/

E. ADDITIONAL RESEARCH-RELATED SITES

1. American Evaluation Association

This is an international professional association of evaluators devoted to the application and exploration of program evaluation, personnel evaluation, technology, and other forms of evaluation.

http://www.eval.org/

2. American Fact Finder

In 1996, the U.S. Census undertook a comprehensive multiyear development effort to build a data dissemination system. American Fact Finder uses high-performance computing systems to enable users to select data tabulations and maps from data sets in the system.

http://factfinder.census.gov/

3. American Institutes for Research

The American Institutes for Research (AIR) is an independent, not-for-profit corporation that performs basic and applied research, provides technical support, and conducts analyses in the behavioral and social sciences.

http://www.air.org/

4. American Psychological Association Science Directorate: Testing and Assessment

The American Psychological Association provides answers to frequently asked questions about the selection and use of psychological tests.

http://www.apa.org/science/testing.html

5. American Sociological Association Section on Methods

This website provides information about the activities of the American Sociological Association Section on Methods.

http://www.asanet.org/sections/methodology.cfm

6. ANU-Coombsweb

This archive site was established to act as an electronic repository of social science and humanities papers, bibliographies, directories, abstracts, and other high-grade research material produced (or deposited) at the Research Schools of Social Sciences and Pacific and Asian Studies, Australian National University, Canberra, Australia.

http://coombs.anu.edu.au/

7. Bioethics Resources on the Web

An excellent list of resources about human subjects research and institutional review boards from the National Institutes for Health.

http://www.nih.gov/sigs/bioethics/IRB.html

8. Bureau of Justice Assistance Evaluation Website

The Bureau of Justice Assistance is committed to the importance of program evaluation and to developing and enhancing evaluation capabilities at state and local levels. This website is designed to provide state administrative agency staff, criminal justice planners, researchers, and evaluators, as well as local practitioners, with a variety of resources for evaluating criminal justice programs.

http://www.ojp.usdoj.gov/BJA/evaluation/

9. Buros Institute of Mental Measurements

This comprehensive site provides reviews of tests, links to important resources for testing, and standards for utilization tests.

http://www.unl.edu/buros/

10. Campbell Collaboration

The international Campbell Collaboration (C2) is a nonprofit organization that aims to help people make well-informed decisions about the effects of interventions in the social, behavioral, and educational arenas. Its major products are publications that include systematic reviews and methodological guidelines.

http://www.campbellcollaboration.org/

11. Catalyst

This offers an exclusive focus on leadership, education, and research. Individuals around the world can be equipped with the skills and insights to achieve creative ways of leading groups and organizations.

http://www.catalyst.org/

12. Center for Creative Leadership

This offers individuals an exclusive focus on leadership, education, research, and expertise in solving the leadership challenges of individuals and organizations.

http://www.ccl.org/leadership/index.aspx

13. Center for Demography and Ecology

The Center for Demography and Ecology (CDE) is a multi-disciplinary faculty research cooperative for social scientific demographic research whose membership includes sociologists, rural sociologists, economists, and historians.

http://www.ssc.wisc.edu/cde/

14. Center for Social Research Methods

This website, developed by Bill Trochim at Cornell, is intended for people involved in applied social research and evaluation. There are many links to other locations on the web that deal in applied social research methods, previously published and unpublished papers, detailed examples of current research projects, useful tools for researchers (like a guide to selecting a statistical analysis), an extensive online textbook, a bulletin board for discussions, and more.

http://www.socialresearchmethods.net/

15. Cochrane Collaboration

The Cochrane Collaboration is an international nonprofit and independent organization dedicated to making up-to-date, accurate information about the effects of health care readily available worldwide. Its major products are published systematic reviews and methodological guidelines.

http://www.cochrane.org

16. Community of Science

The mission of the Community of Science (COS) is to provide rapid, easy-to-use information about scientists and the funding of science. The COS is a global registry designed to provide accurate, timely, easy-to-access information about what new funding opportunities exist and who is working on what subject and where.

http://www.cos.com/

17. Council on Contemporary Families

The Council on Contemporary Families (CCF) is a non-profit, nonpartisan organization dedicated to informing the public of the latest research and best-practice findings about American families. Members include demographers, economists, family therapists, historians, political scientists, psychologists, social workers, and sociologists, as well as other family social scientists and practitioners.

http://www.contemporaryfamilies.org/

18. Economic & Social Research Council

The Economic & Social Research Council (ESRC) Society Today is a new website offering access to an unrivaled range of high-quality social and economic research. It is run by the ESRC, the U.K.'s largest funding agency for research and postgraduate training relating to social and economic issues.

http://www.esrc.ac.uk/ESRCInfoCentre/index_academic
.aspx

19. The Foundation Finder

Foundation Finder allows users to search by grant maker name, including former, partial, and common names. Search geographically to identify grant makers in a given city, state, or zip code, or search by EIN number.

http://lnp.foundationcenter.org/finder.html

20. Human Rights Campaign

The Human Rights Campaign (HRC) is the largest U.S. civil rights organization working to achieve lesbian, gay, bisexual, and transgender (LGBT) equality. HRC strives to end discrimination against LGBT citizens and realize a nation that achieves fundamental fairness and equality for all.

http://www.hrc.org/

21. Idea Works, Inc.

This is an information technology company specializing in the development and publication of expert systems for business, industry, research, and human services.

http://www.ideaworks.com/

22. The Illinois Researcher Information Service

The Illinois Researcher Information Service (IRIS) is a unit of the University of Illinois Library at Urbana-Champaign. The IRIS office compiles the IRIS database of funding opportunities. The office also maintains a library of publications (informational brochures, application guidelines, and annual reports) from more than 2,000 funding agencies.

http://www.library.uiuc.edu/iris/

23. Institute for Social Research

Here, you'll find information about the research facility at the University of Michigan. It includes the Survey Research Center, the Research Center for Group Dynamics, the Population Studies Center, the Center for Political Studies, and the Inter-University Consortium for Political and Social Research.

http://www.isr.umich.edu/

24. Internal Validity Tutorial

This self-instructional tutorial on internal validity teaches students to recognize and analyze flaws in the design of clinical experiments.

http://psych.athabascau.ca/html/Validity/

25. International Mothers Network

The International Mothers Network (IMN) is a global consortium of more than 50 mothering organizations committed to a more mother-centered world, dedicated to bringing diverse mothers' groups together to work toward influencing public discussion, as well as exploring alternate economic and societal structures.

http://www.internationalmothersnetwork.org/home.html

26. Internet Resources for Institutional Research

Here are links to assist institutional researchers, faculty, and students in higher education in navigating the Internet.

http://airweb.org/links/

27. Joanna Briggs Institute

The Joanna Briggs Institute is an international not-for-profit research and development organization specializing in evidence-based resources for health care professionals in nursing, midwifery, medicine, and allied health. With more than 54 centers and groups servicing more than 90 countries, the Joanna Briggs Institute is a recognized global leader in evidence-based health care.

http://www.joannabriggs.edu.au/

28. Mathematica Policy Research, Inc.

Mathematica Policy Research, Inc. has been known for its high-quality, objective research to support decisions about our nation's most pressing social policy problems. The firm has conducted some of the most important studies of health care, welfare, education, employment, nutrition, and early childhood policies and programs in the United States.

http://www.mathematica-mpr.com/

29. National Council for Research on Women

The National Council for Research on Women (NCRW) is a network of 120 leading research, policy, and advocacy centers dedicated to improving the lives of women and girls by providing the latest news, analysis, and strategies needed to ensure fully informed debates, effective policies, and inclusive practices.

http://www.ncrw.org/

30. National Council on Family Relations

The National Council on Family Relations (NCFR) provides an educational forum for family researchers, educators, and practitioners to share in the development and dissemination of knowledge about families and family relationships. It also establishes professional standards and works to promote general family well-being.

http://www.ncfr.org/

31. National Institutes of Health Funding Opportunities

This includes information about National Institutes of Health (NIH) grant and fellowship programs, applying for grants or fellowships, policy changes, administrative responsibilities of awardees, the CRISP database, and the numbers and characteristics of awards made by the NIH.

http://grants.nih.gov/grants/

32. On Being a Scientist: Responsible Conduct in Research

This is an online publication of the Committee of Science, Engineering, and Public Policy of the National Academy of Sciences.

http://www.nap.edu/readingroom/books/obas/

33. OpinionMeter

This is an interactive, fully automated polling machine to measure customer satisfaction.

http://www.opinionmeter.com/

34. Parents Anonymous

Parents Anonymous is the nation's oldest and largest child abuse prevention organization dedicated to strengthening families through innovative strategies that promote mutual support and parent leadership.

http://www.parentsanonymous.org/

35. Partnership for a Drug-Free America

This site includes a comprehensive database of drug information: what they do, what they look like, their history, and slang terms.

http://www.drugfree.org

36. Power Calculator

This web-based software determines statistical power.
http://calculators.stat.ucla.edu/powercalc/

37. Qualitative Methods (QualPage)

Here are resources for qualitative researchers.
http://www.qualitativeresearch.uga.edu/QualPage/

38. RAND

Through research and analysis, RAND assists public policy-makers at all levels, private sector leaders in many industries, and the public at large in efforts to strengthen the nation's economy, maintain its security, and improve its quality of life.

http://www.rand.org/

39. Research Navigator

Research Navigator is designed to help you with the research process with everything from identifying a topic to editing a text. It also accesses four databases including the EBSCO Academic Journal and Abstract Database, *New York Times* Search by Subject Archive, the Best of the Web Link Library, and *Financial Times* article archives and company financials.

http://www.researchnavigator.com

40. Russell Sage Foundation

The principal American foundation devoted exclusively to research in the social sciences, the foundation is a research center, a funding source for studies by scholars at other academic and research institutions, and an active member of the nation's social science community.

http://www.russellsage.org/

41. Social Science Information Gateway

The Social Science Information Gateway (SOSIG) aims to provide a trusted source of selected, high-quality Internet information for researchers and practitioners in the social sciences, business, and law. It is part of the U.K. Resource Discovery Network.

http://sosig.esrc.bris.ac.uk/

42. Social Science Research Center

The Social Science Research Center (SSRC) at Mississippi State University makes available many of their research reports on this site.

http://www.ssrc.msstate.edu/

43. Society for Judgment and Decision Making

The Society for Judgment and Decision Making is an inter-disciplinary organization dedicated to the study of norma-tive, descriptive, and prescriptive theories of decision.

http://www.sjdm.org/

44. Society for Social Work and Research

The Society for Social Work and Research (SSWR) is a dis-ciplinary association of individuals interested in promoting and disseminating high-quality research in the field of social work. It is primarily composed of social work academics, graduate students, and, to a lesser extent, practitioners. It sponsors several research journals available as a benefit to its members, supports an annual research conference, and advocates at the federal level for enhanced attention and funding of social work research.

http://www.sswr.org

45. Sociologists for Women in Society

An international organization of sociologists and social scientists, these professionals work together to improve the position of women in both sociology and society.

http://www.socwomen.org/

46. StatCenter

StatCenter is a set of diverse resources for teaching and learning introductory statistics over the web. It is not a stand-alone course that teaches statistics and delivers credit. It is meant to support teachers and students with already existing classes.

http://www.utah.edu/stat/

47. StatLib

StatLib is a system for distributing statistical software, data sets, and information by e-mail, FTP, and on the World Wide Web. It is a service of the Carnegie Mellon University Statistics Department.

http://lib.stat.cmu.edu/

48. Statistical Resources on the Internet

This site provides as a starting point for locating statistics-related information on the World Wide Web.

http://www.stat.vt.edu/links.htm

49. The American National Election Study

The American National Election Study (ANES) produces high-quality data on voting, public opinion, and political participation; researchers can download data sets on election studies conducted between 1952 and 2004.

http://www.electionstudies.org/

50. The Electronic Statistical Textbook

This Electronic Statistical Textbook offers training in the understanding and application of statistics.

http://www.statsoftinc.com/textbook/stathome.html

51. The University Center for Urban and Social Research

Established at University of Pittsburgh to carry out basic and applied social science research, the University Center for Social and Urban Research (UCSUR) is a focal point for collaborative interdisciplinary and multidisciplinary approaches to social science and policy issues.

http://www.ucsur.pitt.edu/

52. The World Wide Web Virtual Library: Statistics

This is a cornucopia of links related to statistics. It is easy to understand and use.

http://www.stat.ufl.edu/vlib/statistics.html

CHAPTER 5

CORE DISCIPLINARY JOURNALS IN SELECTED SOCIAL AND BEHAVIORAL SCIENCES

Often, students review published articles in professional journals usually found in university libraries. Reviews of literature, appraisals of various search engines, and a variety of information for retrieval is virtually at any student's fingertips. In any profession, there is a series of main journals that members of that profession deem to be more prestigious or important to their particular field. These are often called Tier 1 or core journals in the field. They are found in the *Journal Citation Reports*, published by the *Web-of-Science—Social Science Version*. In these sites, articles are reviewed and ranked by the number of times they are cited yearly. This way, students can look at which journals are most frequently cited by individuals in their respective fields of study. Here, we list the 13 discipline-specific journals ranked by the *Web-of-Science* site from 2008. We included a few other well-cited journals here and also ones that only have URLs so you can hotlink them at your pleasure. Journals not in your discipline list either were not well cited by other authors in these rankings or did not have URL links. Hopefully, students will broaden their research acumen by exploring these journals in their respective disciplines.

A. Social Work

Social Work—http://www.naswpress.org/publications/journals/sw.html

Research on Social Work Practice—http://rsw.sagepub.com/

British Journal of Social Work—http://bjsw.oxfordjournals.org/

Social Service Review—http://www.journals.uchicago.edu/toc/ssr/current

Journal of Social Work Education—http://www.naswpress.org/publications/journals/swr.htm

Health and Social Work—http://www.naswpress.org/publications/journals/hsw.html

Social Work Research—http://www.naswpress.org/publications/journals/swr.html

Families in Society—http://www.familiesinsociety.org/

Child Welfare—http://www.cwla.org/articles/cwjabstracts.htm

International Journal of Social Welfare—http://www.wiley.com/bw/journal.asp?ref=1369-6866

Australian Social Work—http://www3.interscience.wiley.com/journal/118654853/home?CRETRY=1&SRETRY=0

Canadian Social Work Review—http://www.caswe-acfts.ca/en/Canadian_Social_Work_Review_32.html

B. Sociology

American Sociological Review—http://www.asanet.org/journals/asr/

American Journal of Sociology—http://www.journals.uchicago.edu/toc/ajs/current

Annual Review of Sociology—http://www.annualreviews
.org/journal/soc

Sociological Methodology—http://www.jstor.org/action/
showPublication?journalCode=socimeth

Social Networks—http://arjournals.annualreviews.org/toc/
soc/35/1

Social Problems—http://ucpressjournals.com/journal
.asp?j=sp

Sociology of Health and Illness—http://www
.blackwellpublishing.com/shil_enhanced/

British Journal of Sociology—http://www2.1se.ac.uk/BJS/
Home.aspx

Canadian Journal of Sociology—http://ejournals.library
.ualberta.ca/index.php/CJS/

Population and Development Review—http://www3
.interscience.wiley.com/journal/117976239/home

C. Psychology

Annual Review of Psychology—http://arjournals
.annualreviews.org/loi/psych

Psychological Bulletin—http://www.apa.org/pubs/journals/
bul/index.asp

Psychological Review—http://www.apa.org/pubs/journals/
bul/index.aspx

American Psychologist—http://www.apa.org/pubs/journals/
amp/index.aspx

Journal of Abnormal Psychology—http://www.apa.org/
pubs/journals/abn/index.aspx

Clinical Psychology Review—http://www.sciencedirect.com/
science/journal/02727358

Journal of Consulting and Clinical Psychology—http://
www.apa.org/pubs/journals/ccp/index.aspx

British Journal of Psychology—http://www.bpsjournals
   .co.uk/journals/bjp/

Psychological Science—http://www.wiley.com/bw/journal
   .asp?ref=0956-7976

Australian Journal of Psychology—http://www.tandf.co.uk/
   journals/titles/00049530.asp

D. Education

Review of Educational Research—http://www.aera.net/
   publications/?id=319

Journal of Educational and Behavioral Statistics—
   http://jebs.aera.net/

America Educational Research Journal—http://aer.sagepub.com/

Educational Evaluation and Policy Analysis—http://eepa
   .aera.net/

Journal of Experimental Education—http://www.heldref
   .org/pubs/jxe/about.html

Review of Research in Education—http://rre.aera.net/

Review of Educational Research—http://rer.aera.net/

British Educational Research Journal—http://www
   .informaworld.com/smpp/title~content=t713406264

Canadian Journal of Education—http://www.csse.ca/CJE/
   General.htm

Australian Journal of Education—http://www.acer.edu.au/
   press/aje

E. Nursing

International Journal of Nursing Studies—http://www
   .heldref.org/pubs/jxe/about.html

Journal of Advanced Nursing—http://www
   .journalofadvancednursing.com/

Nursing Research—http://journals.lww.com/
nursingresearchonline/pages/default.aspx

Journal of Clinical Nursing—http://www3.interscience
.wiley.com/journal/118513605/home

Evidence-Based Nursing—http://ebn.bmj.com/

Advances in Nursing Science—http://journals.lww.com/
advancesinnursingscience/pages/default.aspx

Canadian Journal of Nursing Research—http://cjnr
.mcgill.ca/

British Journal of Nursing—http://www
.britishjournalofnursing.com/

Australian Journal of Advanced Nursing—http://www.ajan
.com.au/

F. Criminology

Criminology—http://www.wiley.com/bw/journal
.asp?ref=0011-1384

Journal of Research in Crime and Delinquency—http://jrc
.sagepub.com/

Criminal Justice and Behavior—http://cjb.sagepub.com/

Crime and Delinquency—http://www.sagepub.com/
journalsProdDesc.nav?prodId=Journal200959

Journal of Quantitative Criminology—http://www.springer
.com/social+sciences/criminology/journal/10940

Justice Quarterly—http://www.ingentaconnect.com/content/
routledg/rjqy

British Journal of Criminology—http://bjc.oxfordjournals
.org/

Journal of Criminal Justice—http://www.elsevier
.com/wps/find/journaldescription.cws_home/366/
description#description

Canadian Journal of Criminology & Criminal Justice—http://www.ccja-acjp.ca/en/cjc2/cjc52s1.html

Australian and New Zealand Journal of Criminology—http://www.australianacademicpress.com.au/ Publications/Journals/Criminology/Criminology.htm

G. Family Studies

Journal of Sex and Marital Therapy—http://www.tandf.co.uk/journals/titles/0092623x.asp

Journal of Family Psychology—http://www.apa.org/pubs/journals/fam/index.aspx

Child Abuse and Neglect—http://www.elsevier.com/wps/find/journaldescription.authors/586/description

Child Maltreatment—http://cmx.sagepub.com/

Journal of Marriage and the Family—http://www.wiley.com/bw/journal.asp?ref=0022-2445

Family Relations—http://www3.interscience.wiley.com/journal/117997753/home

Family Process—http://www3.interscience.wiley.com/journal/117959054/home

Journal of Marital and Family Therapy—http://www.jmft.net/

The Australian and New Zealand Journal of Family Therapy—http://www.anzjft.com/pages/sample_articles.php

Journal of Family Therapy—http://www3.interscience.wiley.com/journal/118494276/home

H. Counseling

Journal of Counseling Psychology—http://www.apa.org/pubs/journals/cou/

Journal of Mental Health Counseling—http://www.amhca.org/news/journal.aspx

Journal of College Student Psychotherapy—
   http://www.informaworld.com/smpp/
   title~content=t792303990~db=all

Counseling Outcome Research and Evaluation—
   http://www.sagepub.com/journalsProdDesc
   .nav?prodId=Journa1201967&

*Measurement and Evaluation in Counseling and
   Development*—http://www.sagepub.com/
   journalsProdDesc.nav?prodId=Journa1201951&

The Counseling Psychologist—http://www.sagepub.com/
   journalsProdDesc.nav?prodId=Journa1200805&

British Journal of Guidance and Counseling—http://www
   .tandf.co.uk/journals/carfax/03069885.html

Canadian Journal of Counseling—http://cjc
   .synergiesprairies.ca/cjc/index.php/rcc

Professional School Counseling Journal—http://www
   .schoolcounselor.org/content.asp?contentid=235

Australian Journal of Guidance and Counseling—
   http://www.australianacademicpress.com.au/
   Publications/Journals/Guidance&Counselling/
   guidecounsel.htm

American Journal of Pastoral Counseling—
   http://www.informaworld.com/smpp/
   title~db=all~content=t904095356

I. Public Health

Annual Review of Public Health—http://arjournals
   .annualreviews.org/loi/publhealth

American Journal of Public Health—http://ajph
   .aphapublications.org/

Tobacco Control—http://tobaccocontrol.bmj.com/

American Journal of Epidemiology—http://aje
   .oxfordjournals.org/

Public Health Ethics—http://phe.oxfordjournals.org/

Journal of Public Health—http://jpubhealth.oxfordjournals
    .org/

European Journal of Public Health—http://eurpub
    .oxfordjournals.org/

Journal of Epidemiology and Community Health—
    http://jech.bmj.com/

Australian and New Zealand Journal of Public Health—
    http://www.wiley.com/bw/journal.asp?ref=1326-0200

Canadian Journal of Public Health—http://www.cpha.ca/en/
    cjph.aspx

J. Political Science

European Journal of Political Science—http://www.wiley
    .com/bw/journal.asp?ref=1326-0200

American Journal of Political Science—http://www.wiley
    .com/bw/journal.asp?ref=0092-5853

Public Opinion Quarterly—http://poq.oxfordjournals.org/

Annual Review of Political Science—http://arjournals
    .annualreviews.org/loi/polisci

American Political Science Review—http://www.apsanet
    .org/content_3222.cfm

British Journal of Political Science—http://journals
    .cambridge.org/action/displayJournal?jid=JPS

Canadian Journal of Political Science—http://journals
    .cambridge.org/action/displayJournal?jid=CJP

Australian Journal of Political Science—http://www.tandf
    .co.uk/journals/titles/10361146.asp

European Journal of Political and Economic Studies—
    http://www.ejeps.com/

European Political Science Review—http://journals
    .cambridge.org/action/displayJournal?jid=EPR

K. Public Administration

Journal of European Public Policy—http://www.tandf
.co.uk/journals/routledge/13501763.html

Journal of Public Administration Research & Theory—
http://jpart.oxfordjournals.org/

Public Administration Review—http://www.wiley.com/bw/
journal.asp?ref=0033-3352

American Review of Public Administration—http://arp
.sagepub.com/

Canadian Public Administration—http://www.wiley.com/
bw/journal.asp?ref=0008-4840

The Innovation Journal—http://www.innovation.cc/

Public Administration and Development—http://www3
.interscience.wiley.com/journal/2821/home

International Journal of Public Administration—
http://www.tandf.co.uk/journals/lpad

Australian Journal of Public Administration—
http://www.wiley.com/bw/journal.asp?ref=0313-6647

*African Journal of Public Administration and
Management*—http://www.aapam.org/Journal.html

L. Business

Academy of Management Journal—http://journals
.aomonline.org/amj/

Academic Management Review—http://www.aom.pace
.edu/amr/

Journal of Retailing—http://www.elsevier.com/
wps/find/journaldescription.cws_home/620186/
description#description

Journal of Marketing—http://www.elsevier.com/wps/
find/journaldescription.cws_home/620186/descript
on#description

Strategic Management Review—http://www
    .strategicmanagementreview.com/ojs/index.php/smr

Marketing Science—http://mktsci.journal.informs.org/

Business and Society—http://www.sagepub.com/
    journalsProdDesc.nav?prodId=Journa1200878

Journal of Management—http://www.sagepub.com/
    journalsProdManSub.nav?prodId=Journa1201724

British Journal of Management—http://www.wiley.com/bw/
    journal.asp?ref=1045-3172

Canadian Journal of Administrative Sciences—http://www3
    .interscience.wiley.com/journal/114269012/home

M. Communication Studies

Journal of Communication—http://www.wiley.com/bw/
    journal.asp?ref=0021-9916

Journal of Communications—http://www
    .academypublisher.com/jcm/

International Journal of Communication—http://ijoc.org/
    ojs/index.php/ijoc

Human Communication Research—http://www.wiley.com/
    bw/journal.asp?ref=0360-3989

Communication Research—http://crx.sagepub.com/

Communication Theory—http://www.wiley.com/bw/
    journal.asp?ref=1050-3293

Journal of Health Communication—http://www.gwu
    .edu/~cih/journal/

European Journal of Communication—http://ejc.sagepub
    .com/

Journal of Applied Communication Research—http://www
    .tandf.co.uk/journals/rjac

Canadian Journal of Communication—http://www
    .cjc-online.ca/index.php/journal

ABOUT THE AUTHORS

Michael J. Holosko, PhD, MSW, is the Pauline M. Berger Professor of Family and Child Welfare at the University of Georgia, School of Social Work, and adjunct instructor at Norfolk State University. He has taught across the undergraduate and graduate curriculum in schools of social work (primarily), nursing, public administration, and applied social science in Canada, the United States, Hong Kong, Sweden, Australia, and the U.S. Virgin Islands. He has published extensively in the areas of evaluation, health care, gerontology, social policy, research, music intervention, and spirituality. For the past 30 years, he has been a consultant to a variety of large and small health and human service organizations in the areas of program evaluation, outcomes, accreditation, organizational development, communication, leadership, visioning, organizational alignment, and stress management. He has published numerous monographs, chapters, articles, and texts in the areas of evaluation, health care, gerontology, social policy, research, music intervention, and spirituality. He serves on the editorial boards of *Research on Social Work Practice; Journal of Health and Social Policy; Journal of Human Behavior and Social Environment;* the *Hong Kong Journal of Social Work; Journal of Social Service Research;* and the *Journal of Evidence-Based Social Work Practice.* For a number of years, he has had both radio and television shows advocating for social justice in North America. His curriculum vita is available online at http://ssw.uga.edu:8091/plone/faculty-staff/directory/mholosko.

Bruce A. Thyer, PhD, LCSW, BCBA, is Professor and former Dean with the College of Social Work at Florida State University. Previously, he held the position of Distinguished Research Professor at the University of Georgia, School of Social Work, and served as a visiting Professor with the University of Huddersfield, England, and with Yonsei University, in Seoul, Republic of Korea. Dr. Thyer is the editor of the bimonthly journal *Research on Social Work Practice* and one of the founders of the Society for Social Work and Research. He has served on the Board of Directors of the Council on Social Work Education, the Council of Representatives of the American Psychological Association, and the Steering Committee of the Group for the Advancement of Doctoral Education in Social Work. He is well published in the areas of research, evaluation, evidence-based practice, research writing and publication, and clinical practice. He holds the LCSW and BCBA (Board Certified Behavior Analyst) practice credentials. His scholarly interests are in the fields of clinical social work, behavior analysis, evidence-based practice, program evaluation, and the role of theory in social work. His curriculum vita is online at http://csw.fsu.edu/staff_pages/thyer.php.